# THE CASE FOR CANNABIS
# LAW REFORM

# THE CASE FOR CANNABIS LAW REFORM

## VINCE McLEOD

First edition – published October 2019

Text © Vince McLeod 2019

Cover design and typesetting by Alan Bridgland @ The CopyPress, Nelson, NZ

ISBN: 978-1-080-97674-4

Please contact vjmpublishing@gmail.com or see our company page at
www.vjmpublishing.nz for more information

# Contents

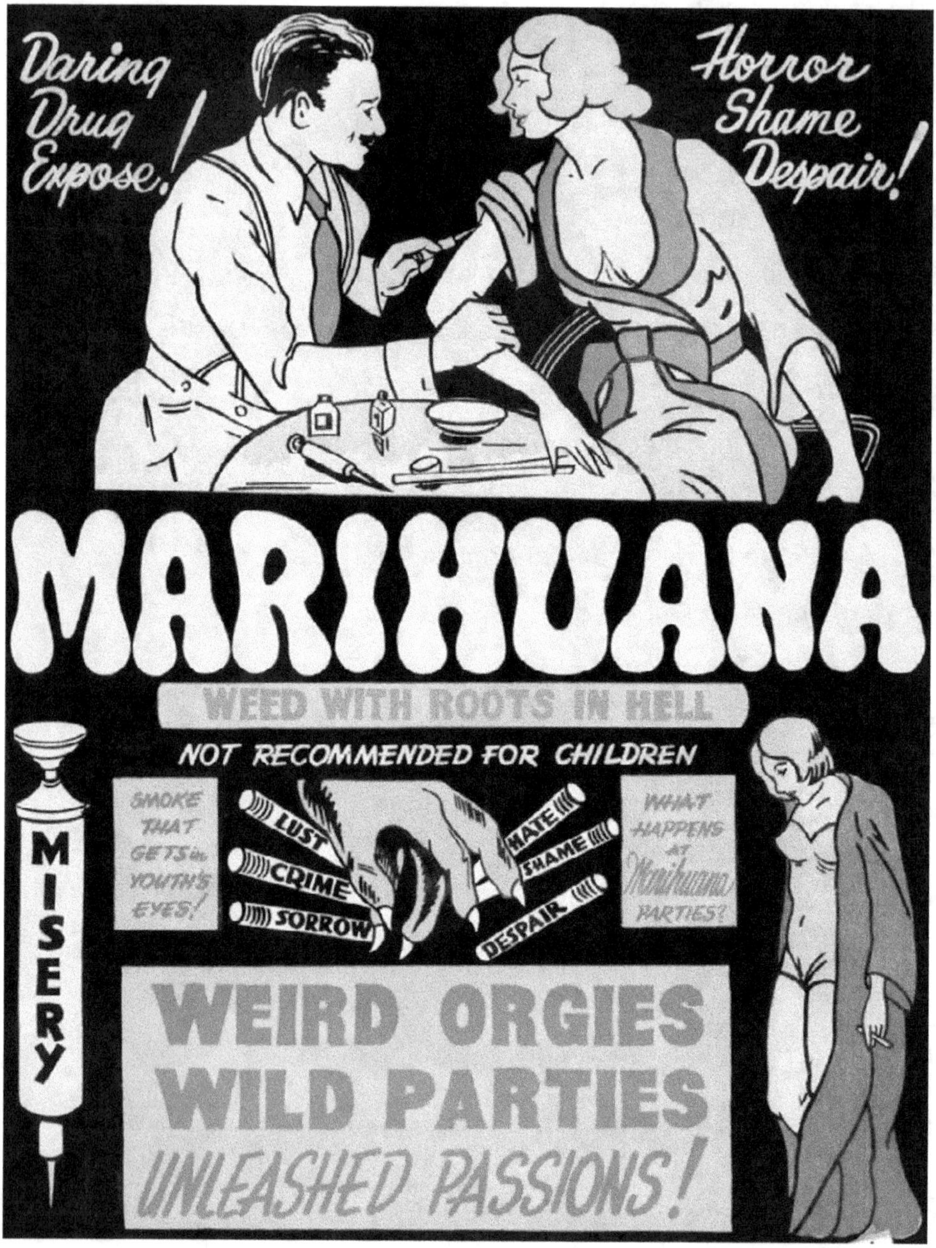

# Introduction

The first time I spoke to a properly informed doctor about cannabis was in 2008, in Los Angeles, on my way back from Europe. His office was adorned in the typically American style, with certificates all over the walls. It was a hot afternoon, and the sidewalk on the ground floor below bustled with roller skaters and tourists.

I explained to him my situation. Without going into too much detail, I explained how I had been bedeviled since childhood by a psychiatric condition that made both sleeping and holding down food very difficult. This condition had wrecked my life, on account of that neither a steady job nor a steady relationship were possible while either persisted.

"Very common," he said. "Insomnia and nausea are two of the main reasons I prescribe cannabis."

I explained that my head was often full of noise, and worst when I lay down to sleep. At that time I could hear people screaming, something which had always kept me from going to bed if I could avoid it. I had found, through crude experimentation, that some strains were helpful for this condition and got me to sleep, whereas others tended to wind me up and be weird.

"What you want to avoid are strains high in THC," he replied. "You want a strain high in CBD."

I said that I was only vaguely aware that a difference existed, but he was happy to explain it to me. THC was useful for some conditions, but not for others, as it wasn't particularly relaxing. Strains that were high in CBD would be much better for the symptoms that I had described.

This all sounded very good, and it was apparent that the doctor knew what he was talking about, and not only was he deeply familiar with the literature but his knowledge was up-to-date. The problem, of course, was that I was going back to New Zealand, where medicinal cannabis was illegal. I wasn't sure that it would ever become legal in New Zealand.

"There are over ten thousand entries for medicinal cannabis on Google Scholar," he pointed out. "The evidence is overwhelming."

This was also the last time I spoke to a properly informed doctor, as all of my doctor's visits since then have been in New Zealand.

To say that the New Zealand authorities have been slow to understand and accept the truth about cannabis is an understatement. The mental health workers I spoke to in the years after returning to New Zealand were very much still in the *Reefer Madness* mindset, where cannabis caused mental illness and all cannabis was the same. A psychiatrist I spoke to even believed that it was possible to estimate a person's level of psychosis by measuring the levels of cannabinoids in their urine - a level of quackery that should be consigned to history alongside trepanning and phrenology.

It was in this light that I wrote the *Cannabis Activist's Handbook* in 2013, a book about how to organise and agitate for cannabis law reform. I posted copies of it to any politician I thought might be interested. Official reception for the arguments in that book were lukewarm, but behind the scenes there was a sense that the logic was watertight.

The six years since then have only confirmed what I had been told in California. The medicinal uses of cannabis were legion, and with every passing month, more and more evidence for cannabis law reform mounts up.

Uruguay legalised cannabis across the board in 2013. Colorado followed in 2014. Washington, Oregon, Alaska followed shortly after that. In 2015, Jamaica made it legal to grow up to five plants. In 2016, the Supreme Court of the nation of Georgia ruled that imprisoning a person for a small amount of cannabis was unconstitutional. Chilean and Mexican courts have also ruled that cannabis prohibition is a human rights violation. With every year that passes, the cannabis laws are relaxed somewhere in the world. New Zealand has fallen so far behind that it is a tragedy.

Even Zimbabwe made medicinal cannabis legal before New Zealand did, and they weren't even the first place in Southern Africa. At time of writing, it's legal for South Africans to cultivate cannabis on their own property - a right that Kiwis are not yet allowed. New Zealanders have fewer rights than several Third World countries when it comes to using cannabis.

Despite the fact that even governments and medical communities in Southern Africa have the background knowledge to understand the truth about cannabis, the New Zealand Establishment has not budged a millimetre. It's still all but impossible to have an properly informed conversation with a doctor in New Zealand about medicinal cannabis. Either they are woefully unaware of the medicinal uses of cannabis or too afraid of the professional consequences of being open about what they know.

Although people in New Zealand are some of the world's most enthusiastic users of cannabis, our supposed authorities have been pathetically slow to inform themselves of the truth about it. Talking to mental health professionals or politicians about it is still much like bashing one's head against a brick wall.

So it's in this light that I have written *The Case For Cannabis Law Reform*.

What I hope is that, from reading this book, both open-minded and skeptical people can come to understand the truth about cannabis, which is that it should not be prohibited. The sum total of human suffering in the world would be less if cannabis were legal, and we should make it so without any further ado.

I believe this book answers every reasonable objection that a person could have to wanting to reform the cannabis laws.

Vince McLeod
Nelson, New Zealand
20 July 2019

# 1

# Prohibition Doesn't Work

Although this book is full of arguments for cannabis law reform, all of them are technically forms of one great meta-argument. All of the arguments for cannabis law reform, as the reader will discover, explore different facets of the failure of cannabis prohibition. The fundamental argument at the core of the case for cannabis law reform is simply that prohibition doesn't work.

Although there are a plethora of different kinds of cannabis law reform, all of them are based on the recognition that cannabis prohibition has a number of costs that could be saved. Although it's denied by many, prohibition does have costs – the cost of law enforcement, the cost of prisons, the cost of faith in the Government, the Police and the medical establishment, among others.

Therefore, in order for this cost to be justified, cannabis prohibition has to do something good. There have to be profits somewhere to make up for all the costs. If there aren't, then cannabis prohibition is a failed experiment and must be ended.

So let us ask: what is the objective of cannabis prohibition?

If the objective was to prevent people from using cannabis, that has failed. In 2008, 14.6 percent of the New Zealand population (1) had used cannabis within the past 12 months, which is comparable to the prevalence rate of tobacco use. A decade later, cannabis is even more popular than before, and tobacco even less.

No intelligent person seriously believes that the law can override the people's will to use cannabis. Exactly like alcohol prohibition, which failed to stop people from using alcohol, cannabis prohibition won't stop people from using cannabis. Not only do people have a will to use it, but they feel that they have the right to do so. They're going to keep using it forever.

If the objective was to protect people's mental health, that too has failed. Not only is there no correlation between rates of cannabis use and prevalence of mental illness on the national level, but there is ample scientific evidence that cannabis does not cause psychosis or schizophrenia (2). The cannabis-psychosis link is best explained by the fact that cannabis is medicinal for many mentally ill people, and so they seek it out.

Instead of protecting people's mental health, cannabis prohibition leads to the further social isolation of cannabis users by making them unwilling to speak candidly to mental health professionals, or to their friends or workmates. If cannabis is illegal, then confessing to using it is tantamount to confessing to criminal activity, so many mentally ill people who need help would rather just sit in silence.

If the objective was to protect children from psychoactive drugs while their brains are still developing, that too has failed. Because cannabis is on the black market, and therefore sold by criminals, there is nothing in the way of age checks between young people and the cannabis supply. Gang members will happily sell bags of cannabis to 12-year olds if they have the cash.

People often make the "think of the children!" argument when it comes to cannabis law reform, but the simple fact is that prohibition makes it easier for minors to get hold of cannabis. Proof for this is as simple as asking a minor if it's easier to get hold of alcohol or cannabis. They'll tell you that it's harder to get hold of booze because those selling it are serious about keeping their liquor license.

If the objective was to instill respect for authority, that's completely backfired. Cannabis prohibition is so stupid an idea that the people at large have lost respect for those pushing it and those enforcing it. Although the idea that one's politicians are stupid and evil is far from new, these sentiments become problematic when they're applied to other segments of society. Prohibition, however, makes this all but inevitable.

Many New Zealanders have now come to feel that the Police are their enemy, because Police officers have shown themselves willing to confiscate people's medicine and to imprison them for using it. Far from being the trusted community servants that they are seen as in places like Holland, they're seen as enemy soldiers waging an immoral war against an innocent people. To a great extent, this is the fault of cannabis prohibition.

All of these arguments (among others) are discussed at length in the various chapters of this book, but they all support the central thesis – that cannabis prohibition doesn't work. It doesn't achieve its stated aim of reducing the sum total of human suffering, and if it doesn't achieve its stated aims, then it isn't justified to continue with it any longer.

The men who pushed cannabis prohibition (3) on a naive and unsuspecting public almost a century ago are now dead. Whether they knew they were speaking falsehoods or whether they were genuinely misled is no longer material. The right thing for us to do is to assess reality accurately, so that we can move forward in the correct direction.

If we look around the world honestly, it's obvious that prohibition has failed. Not only is cannabis culture thriving, even in the most unlikely places, but support for cannabis law reform is rising almost universally, across all nations and demographics. The most striking sign is the ever-increasing number of states, territories or countries (4) that have recently liberalised their cannabis laws.

The cynic might say that this is an example of the bandwagon fallacy, but that is not an accurate criticism. The reason why so many countries are changing their cannabis laws is because the evidence against cannabis prohibition has now mounted so high that it can no longer be ignored. There are now many countries liberalising their cannabis laws for the simple reason that the evidence suggests that it's a better approach.

Cannabis prohibition doesn't work. There is nowhere in the world that has prohibited cannabis and observed any result other than more poverty, distrust, misery and hatred. It's fundamentally for this reason that the cannabis laws ought to be reformed.

# 2

# The Market Needs
# To Be Regulated

One of the strongest arguments for cannabis law reform is the appeal to regulate the market. The idea that a government can make cannabis illegal and then it just "goes away" is childish, and the historical example has borne this out. Legal cannabis is the only realistic way to regulate the market.

Many people envision that the world before cannabis prohibition was one of chaos. Shady dealers set up outside high schools to sell to pupils, pharmacists pushed untested and unresearched cannabis products on a naive public and criminal enterprises got fat with the income from cannabis bootlegging. The reality is closer to the reverse of this.

When a substance such as cannabis becomes illegal by act of law, what that means in practice is that the manufacture and supply of that good becomes completely unregulated. Making something illegal is not a way of regulating it – it's a way of putting it into the "too hard" basket. It shifts control from the regulators to the black market.

The black market doesn't attract nice people. It generally attracts people with no better options – desperados. Because there is currently no opportunity to legally profit from cannabis in New Zealand, the only people who deal with the subject matter are black marketeers. There is no guarantee that such individuals will adhere to what have been established overseas as professional industry standards for the manufacture and supply of cannabis products.

Regarding the manufacture of goods on the black market, it's apparent that there are little in the way of health and safety considerations. This is a relatively minor concern in the case of cannabis, but it's still possible that any bud manufactured by a criminal enterprise has had unwanted chemicals used in the growing process. They might have used chemical fertilisers that leave side-products that people don't want in their bodies, or treated the bud with something to make it appear danker (see Chapter 24).

When it comes to supply, the situation is even worse. A normal business primarily competes with others through advertising, whether word-of-mouth or commercial. They don't compete through intimidation. The manager of the local Countdown would never send an underling to take out Fresh Choice workers for selling on the wrong turf. Black marketeers selling illicit drugs happily take their competitors out such ways, though.

The vast majority of the criminal activity associated with cannabis comes about because of prohibition. It's isn't natural to cannabis. With no regulatory oversight, there's nothing stopping the black market selling to 13-year olds or wiping their competitors out in turf wars. Cannabis is already illegal, so it's not like the victims could go to the Police. Black market actors have free rein until they are arrested.

Practically speaking, there is going to be a cannabis market whether we like it or not, so we might as well make sure that it's on the level.

Regulation would solve the problem of tainted product, because growers will need to be able to account for their grow methodology and process. End consumers will be prevented from becoming ill because the possibility of dangerous chemicals being used at some point in the process will be minimised. If anyone does become sick, responsibility can be placed on the correct party and appropriate measures taken.

Moreover, a regulated cannabis supplier or dealer is much more likely to comply with public requests for decency than the black market is. Regulation will inevitably mean that cannabis dealers will need to become licensed, which means that they are strongly incentivised to adhere to laws regarding not supplying to minors, not supplying to intoxicated people etc. They also can't shoot their competitors and expect that this will lead to a greater market share.

A final benefit is that regulation will mean that cannabis suppliers cannot deal with other products as well. As mentioned elsewhere, the gateway drug effect can only occur (1) when people seeking cannabis are exposed to hard drugs. A professional cannabis retailer will not have an incentive to offer their customers methamphetamine, unlike a gang member. In practice, they are unlikely to even be allowed to sell alcohol or tobacco.

All this means that regulation will have the effect of almost taking cannabis away from the black market entirely. Those who are allowed to compete on the legal market for cannabis will have to meet quality standards that ensure the safety of the users (to such a degree that this is possible when people take psychoactive drugs). This will have the overall effect of reducing harm.

Cannabis should be legal because regulation of cannabis causes less suffering than criminalising it. We need to abandon the childish idea that making something illegal makes it go away, and employ a sophisticated and intelligent approach to dealing with the issues caused by cannabis. The only realistic way to do this is through regulation.

# 3

# People Have A Right To Freedom

All of us take for granted that we are a free people, that we are not slaves and so have the right to autonomy and self-determination. The problem with this line of thinking is that it doesn't survive scrutiny, especially once one asks why we're not allowed to grow or to use cannabis. The libertarian argument is that cannabis ought to be legal for the reason that we are supposed to be a free people.

History shows that the ruling class and the masses are always in conflict over what freedoms that masses are allowed to exercise. Alexei Sayle in *The Young Ones* satirised the cruelty of the medieval ruling class by having a peasant sentenced to death for "whistling on a Tuesday". Although facing the court system for whistling on the wrong day might sound arbitrary, the fact is that it's no more so than cannabis prohibition.

A person does not have to be a libertarian to agree that it is the individual that ultimately has the right to decide what goes into their body. If that person's body is their own private property, then it is that person who decides what goes into it and what doesn't. If that person's body is not their own private property, then whose property is it? If the answer is not their own, then they are a slave.

It doesn't matter if the answer is "the nation" or "the community" because the individual has no way of knowing if the people who claim to be making decisions on behalf of these entities actually are. The vast majority of people can agree that conscription is immoral because it is effectively the Government stating that they own your body, even if you object. If the Government owning your body is immoral in that instance, it is so in other instances.

The argument for freedom is essentially an argument against slavery. What we now call chattel slavery is when the will of a person is entirely subjected to and subjugated by the will of another. If you are a slave, then that other person decides what goes into your body and what does not. This state of subjugation is considered so inhumanly cruel that it is now illegal anywhere that has pretensions to be civilised.

We are forced to ask ourselves, however: is not the prohibition of cannabis, such that if a person presumes to be free enough to grow a cannabis plant in a bucket of dirt then they go to prison for years, in the same category of brutal and unjustified control of another person as chattel slavery?

If we can all agree that freedom entails the right to grow and consume medicinal plants, particularly when neither activity causes harm to anyone, then on what grounds does the Government believe that it has the right to restrict this freedom when it comes to cannabis?

Freedom means freedom. Freedom doesn't mean "You're free to do what you like except for things on this list of arbitrary and inhumane restrictions, because if you do anything on this list you go in a cage".

From the perspective of a cannabis enthusiast, the law prohibiting cannabis is immensely frustrating. It is immensely frustrating to desire cannabis but to not be able to use it because some idiots in Parliament decided that they had the right to decide what goes into your body and not you. This frustration leads to a deep sense of humiliation – sometimes it seems like the main reason for cannabis prohibition is just to rub our faces in it.

Without freedom, depression, low self-esteem and despair follow naturally. It's only natural to lose the will to live when politicians are the ones that decide what goes into your body, because this is a form of authoritarianism. The natural place for authoritarian conduct is between master and slave, or between farmer and livestock – it's not natural for humans to conduct relations between each other on such a level, and the more educated and sophisticated a people are, the less well it works.

There might have been a place for authoritarianism in drug policy a century ago, back when the vast majority of people were illiterate and incapable of rationally forming their own opinions. In such a primitive state, people could not have been expected to handle the complexity of the cannabis issue, and therefore could not have been expected to think rationally about it.

By today, people can simply go on the Internet to find as much information about cannabis as they like. We're able to research the medicinal effects of cannabis, and we're able to research the consequences of legalising cannabis in other places. Every one of us has access to a hundred times more information about cannabis than even Government ministers had as little as ten years ago. We all know that legal restrictions in this area are unreasonable.

Ultimately, cannabis should be legal for people to use because people have the right to be free. There is no higher authority than the individual when it comes to deciding what can and what cannot go into the body of that individual. This means that the law prohibiting this ought to be repealed on the grounds that it is immoral and an unreasonable restriction of our natural right to freedom.

# 4

# God Put Cannabis Here

An uncommon argument for cannabis is that God put it here. This is an uncommon argument on account of the fact that religious sentiments are becoming rarer and rarer, but it has pull even for those who don't follow an organised religion. The argument that God put cannabis here remains a powerful one for some people.

Genesis 1:29 states: "And God said, Behold, I have given you every herb bearing seed, which is upon the face of all the earth…"

It's obvious from reading this, on one of the first pages of the Bible, that according to Christian belief, God created cannabis specifically for the benefit of humans. Cannabis is a herb that bears seed, and we encountered it on the face of the Earth, so therefore a Christian ought to believe that its presence here on Earth is a gift from God that ought to be cherished.

Indeed, it's obvious why a benevolent God would have created such a thing. For someone with the kind of illness that cannabis treats, it can feel like a godsend. Many people with psychological problems have found that cannabis can make the difference between a restful night's sleep and eight hours of torture. For such people, providing cannabis is bound to engender feelings of gratitude.

Is it not true, then, that a human government working to prohibit this medicine, and to make it harder for people to get hold of, is causing people to suffer needlessly, and is therefore doing evil work?

Christians are fond of saying that the world is ruled by Satan, and that the Governments of the world all serve Satan. This will to serve evil is the main reason, they contend, that evil exists. Satan desires to thwart the will of God and to destroy the creation of God, and to cause God's most blessed creation to suffer on account of his infernal envy.

Fair enough, but then why support evil by opposing cannabis law reform? If Satan tricked the rulers of the world into prohibiting a medicine that God had created, why not vote to change it back?

If one opposes legal cannabis, is that not tantamount to saying that God made a mistake by creating cannabis for human use, and that humans know better than God by making it illegal instead? From an Abrahamic perspective, this surely constitutes a grave sin. It's blasphemy to elevate the laws of men above the laws of God.

Christians must believe that cannabis ought to be legal for the reason that God put it here. Cannabis is part of the natural world, and if Christians believe that God created the natural world and saw that it was good, so it must be God's will for humans to use cannabis as needed to avoid suffering.

A reader might object here, and say that this argument is just an example of the naturalistic fallacy. This objection argues that, even if one concedes that God created cannabis, this doesn't mean that we should be using it. After all, we don't eat nightshade berries either, and those are just as much a part of the natural world as cannabis is.

A logical person would agree. Just because cannabis is natural doesn't mean that everyone should necessarily be using it. However – no-one is arguing for this. No-one is arguing that anyone should be forced to use cannabis, or even exposed to it in cases where this exposure would cause suffering. To the contrary, cannabis law reformers would argue that legalisation is better for keeping it out of the hands of the wrong people.

All that cannabis law reformers want is for the Government to stand back and allow them to use a natural plant, something that appears to be just as much a part of creation as the sunlight and the rain, as well as the wheat, apples, kiwifruit, potatoes and all the other plants.

Cannabis ought to be legal because it's a moral obscenity for humans to arrogate to themselves the power to make parts of Nature, elements of God's creation, illegal. There is a scriptural basis for believing that God put cannabis here for the benefit of humans, and anyone who believes in those scriptures surely must also believe that God did not do so in error.

# 5

# Cannabis Is A Medicine

Of all the ways that cannabis prohibition causes harm to people, maybe the worst is how it denies many people an effective medicine. The problem is not just limited to the effect that prohibition has on accessing the substance – prohibition also makes it harder to research it and to learn how to best use it. This has the effect of causing a lot of needless suffering.

Cannabis has been used as a medicine for thousands of years. In fact, as Professor David Nutt wrote this year in the *British Medical Journal*, it's probably the oldest medicine known to humanity (1). Its medicinal effects for treating conditions like depression were known to the scientific literature as far back as 1890 (2).

The fact that cannabis is known to be a medicine today can be demonstrated by going to Google Scholar and typing in "medicinal cannabis". This returns (at time of writing) 44,000 results, which means that there are over 40,000 medical journal articles and papers investigating medicinal cannabis.

Frustratingly, it's possible to go back as far as 2008 and see that there are already 14,100 results for a Google Scholar search for "medicinal cannabis". If one considers that medicinal cannabis was made legal in many American states when even less was known than this, it strikes one how glacial the pace of change has been in New Zealand.

The medical conditions for which cannabis has shown promise include eating difficulties (3), sleeping problems (4), Crohn's disease (5), epilepsy

(6), multiple sclerosis (7), nausea and vomiting (8), pain and wasting syndrome (cachexia) (9) and even mental health conditions like anxiety (10), schizophrenia (11), depression (12), social anxiety disorder (13) and psychosis (14). In chronic pain situations it can lead to less opiate use (15).

The problem is the law. Because of the long-standing prohibitions on cannabis, it's difficult to properly research the substance. For a university research program to conduct a proper study, they need to test the effects of cannabis on a large number of people, in a controlled and replicable environment. This requires getting hold of a large amount of cannabis – very difficult when cannabis is illegal.

Without being able to conduct large trials, it's difficult to collect a sufficient amount of data to pass certain levels of proof. Because of the ever-present threat of charlatanism in the pharmaceutical industry, it has become necessary to demand rigorous testing before a prospective medicine gets governmental approval to be sold. Prohibition makes it harder for cannabis to get that approval.

Despite this, there is still a fair bit known about the medicinal effects of cannabis.

It's acknowledged by honest researchers today (16) that "therapeutic benefits of medicinal cannabis are well documented in the treatment of a variety of medical conditions". The problem is that, because of prohibition, it's impossible to arrive at standardised models of production, distribution and prescription.

This is more of a problem than it might first appear to be.

Without a standardised model of production, it's difficult for doctors to have any confidence in what they're prescribing. Because many medicines have dosage-dependent adverse side-effects, it's important to know exactly what proportions of effective medicine are found in each pill that's being dished out. Impurities are to be avoided. Absent this, it's impossible for a doctor to know what to prescribe.

Without standardised prescription guidelines, it's impossible to know how much to prescribe. It's not just a matter of getting as much cannabis into the patient as possible. Responsible medical practice means being aware of potential side-effects and interactions with other medicines, and how these work with factors like age and body weight. If this knowledge is not present, it might seem wise to err on the side of prudence and ignore cannabis.

After all, even if cannabis prohibition was repealed tomorrow and doctors had access to all the cannabis in the world, they would still need to know how to use it safely before they could feel comfortable prescribing it.

Despite the presence of these hurdles, the fact remains that knowledge of the medicinal applications of cannabis are becoming ever-more widespread. Indeed, even Zimbabwe is aware that cannabis is medicinal. Not only has the impoverished Southern African state had medicinal cannabis since 2017 (17), but their Health Minister is getting praise from other Southern African nations for their relatively forward-thinking stance on the issue (18).

Some might argue that the New Zealand medical establishment has shown itself to be more interested in toeing the legal and bureaucratic line than actually helping their patients, and that their reluctance to deal with what was clearly an important issue for many of their patients was cowardly. This might be true for many doctors. The point, however, is not to apportion blame, but to determine the correct path forward.

The major problem with unlocking the medicinal potential of cannabis is the law. It's the law that keeps researchers and scientists from finding out which applications of cannabis make medicinal sense and which ones don't. Since people are going to use cannabis anyway, it makes sense from a harm reduction perspective to expand our knowledge of the plant. This would make it possible to make better-informed decisions about its use.

Legalising cannabis would restore sanity to the situation. It would allow companies and universities to conduct full-scale trials of medicinal cannabis products. This would allow those medical professionals who are interested in learning about the therapeutic effects of cannabis to have more accurate data upon which to base their prescription decisions.

# 6

# Cannabis Is
# An Established Crop

The War on Cannabis seems to be based on the idea that cannabis, if persecuted hard enough, could potentially be eradicated, so that no-one used it at all anymore. In reality, such a war is unwinnable, for a number of reasons. This chapter will make the argument that cannabis ought to be legal on account of that it is an established crop.

One of the reasons why cannabis prohibition was doomed to failure was because cannabis has been used by people all around the world for thousands of years. Despite the best efforts of prohibitionists to eradicate all knowledge of cannabis cultivation and use, people remain aware of its medicinal properties. Cannabis has been illegal for almost a century, but its medical uses are reflections of the natural world, because the calming, soporific and therapeutic effects are universal to humans.

For this reason, demand will always exist for cannabis, no matter what the law says. Whether by underground chemists, criminals, shamans, botanical scientists, insomnia and nausea sufferers or simply by the curious, cannabis culture has been kept alive despite the massive efforts to eradicate it. It's likely that it always will stay alive, on account of that there are so many people who think so positively of the plant.

Evidence that cannabis is an established crop can be seen from the vast number of popular cultural references to it. Films like *Harold and Kumar Go To White Castle* and *Pineapple Express* base their entire plotlines around the audience understanding cannabis and how it works, and that's without even mentioning Cheech and Chong. There are entire genres of music called things like "stoner rock" or "stoner metal", and literary references to cannabis or its effects are legion.

This establishment is a physical fact as well as a cultural one. All around the world cannabis is being grown, and there are millions of seeds in possession of private growers, who are just waiting for the Government to get out of the way. In every town and city there are rings of people who share seeds, clones and buds. Hundreds of millions of people have a medical condition that might be alleviated by cannabis, and tens of millions of these are aware of the benefits of cannabis and are trying to inform the others.

This demand survived prohibition; it will always be there.

Perhaps the best way of measuring this demand is by measuring the size of the cannabis market. Most people in New Zealand don't understand how big the cannabis market is. Last year, Colorado made $1,500 million worth of cannabis sales (1) to a population roughly the same size as New Zealand, or roughly $300 per person per year. Considering that this is after 90 years of adverse propaganda – in other words, 90 years of fervent abnormalisation of cannabis use – $1.5 billion is a lot of money.

Even without sentiment, in the cold hard light of pure commerce, the argument exists for cannabis to be treated as a major industry simply on account of its size. If the industry is worth billions then it deserves a place at the table alongside other industries of similar size. There ought to be Members of Parliament willing to argue the corner of the cannabis industry, and the consumers served by that industry, like there are for the mining, racing, alcohol and tobacco industries, among others.

Fighting cannabis, and trying to eradicate it from popular culture by means of prohibition, makes as much sense as fighting potatoes. All over the world it's possible to find cannabis enthusiasts who are devoted to the promulgation of their chosen plant and the culture around it. None of these enthusiasts can understand cannabis prohibition – making a plant illegal is insane, however you look at it. They will keep cannabis culture going.

Ultimately, the desire of the people to use cannabis for recreation and for medicine has proven itself stronger than the ability of the ruling class to successfully bullshit the rest of the population into accepting prohibition. Use of the plant is so deeply entrenched in culture worldwide that attempts to get rid of it are futile. Cannabis is here to stay, and the law ought to reflect this.

# 7

# Effectiveness Of The Police

Of all of the side-effects of cannabis prohibition, one of the most insidious is the suffering caused to the population by decreased bureaucratic and institutional effectiveness. This occurs across a range of Government agencies, but none as severely as the criminal justice system. As this chapter will examine, cannabis prohibition makes the Police less effective and less able to do their jobs properly.

A lot of successful Police work depends on input from the community, because the Police frequently rely on tips from people who know about crimes. Criminals aren't always tight-lipped, and sometimes they talk about their crimes when they shouldn't (especially to women). Many more crimes get solved as a result of someone who knew the perpetrator ratting them out than as a result of detectives finding clues with magnifying glasses.

This is why reports of crimes in the media frequently come with an appeal from Police to witnesses or anyone who knows the perpetrator to come forward. Realistically, this is the best that the Police can do in many cases. It's easy to see, then, that policing depends on having good relations with the community, and a sense of mutual trust.

If cannabis is illegal, then any individual cannabis user is going to be very wary of the Police, and for good reason. They will be highly averse to having officers come to their house, and will be highly averse to making contact with the Police. After all, they are criminals themselves.

It's easy to imagine this from the perspective of a cannabis user. Why would a cannabis user who has just witnessed a crime call the Police, when doing so greatly increases the risk that said cannabis user gets arrested themselves? If the Police want to talk to them, then the cannabis user is going to have to present themselves with no sign that they use cannabis, or risk getting arrested.

This makes the Police less effective because they can no longer rely on the voluntary co-operation of cannabis users. Prohibition shifts people who use cannabis from the set of potential Police allies into the set of Police opponents.

This also isn't the only way that cannabis makes the Police less effective.

A British study showed that one million manhours of Police time was spent every year on enforcing cannabis prohibition (1). This accounts for all the arrests, all the time spent booking and processing people and the following up of tips. Adjusting for the size of the country, that suggests that somewhere between 70,000 and 80,000 manhours are wasted in this manner every year in New Zealand.

The fact of the matter is that the general Police budget is limited, and the manhours used to enforce cannabis prohibition come out of that general Police budget. So 70,000 hours spent harassing people for cannabis is 70,000 hours not spent following up burglaries, assaults, thefts and the other petty crimes whose enforcement depends on general funding.

In the wake of the Christchurch mosque shootings, it emerged that shooter Branton Tarrant had never had his firearms licence checked by the Police. He had come to New Zealand with an Australian firearms licence and used that to purchase weaponry, and at no point was it ensured that he had his firearms safely locked away, or even that he was in a sound mind to own them.

This is not to argue that the Christchurch mosque shootings would have been prevented if cannabis was legal. The point is that Police effectiveness is a matter of correctly apportioning their limited manhours to enforcing the laws of New Zealand. Should they decide that a certain amount of spending is necessary to enforce cannabis prohibition, then they cannot escape the opportunity cost of not having the funding to fully enforce certain other areas.

Cannabis prohibition should be repealed for the sake of making the Police force more effective. Not only would this allow for a decrease in the mistrust held by sections of the population towards the Police, but it would also allow them to expend their resources more efficiently, by freeing up at least 70,000 manhours currently wasted every year on enforcing cannabis prohibition.

# 8

# Prohibition Is A Waste Of Money

People often talk about cannabis prohibition as if it was just a law and that was that. The reality is that enforcing cannabis prohibition not only costs a large amount of money, but it also prevents a large amount of money from being made. In fact, cannabis prohibition is a colossal waste of money, so much so that it's worth repealing it on that basis alone.

The cost of cannabis prohibition to New Zealand alone is close to half a billion dollars a year. This is comprised of two groups of costs: the direct cost of enforcing prohibition, and the opportunity cost of prohibition.

The direct cost of enforcing prohibition chiefly includes prison costs, court costs and Police costs.

According to an estimate made by the New Zealand Treasury (1), New Zealand spends about $400,000,000 dollars every year on enforcing cannabis prohibition, and is missing out on $150,000,000 of GST on cannabis sales. This means that, according to the New Zealand Government itself, the opportunity cost of enforcing cannabis prohibition is over half a billion dollars a year.

A study by Harvard economist Jeffrey Miron (2) estimated that the American federal government spends USD8,700,000,000 annually on enforcing cannabis prohibition. Adjusted for population size and currency, this suggests that something in the range of $200,000,000 is spent annually in New Zealand to enforce cannabis prohibition (this includes court and prison costs as well as Police costs).

Potentially much greater than this is the opportunity cost of prohibition.

The Miron report linked above suggested that America loses a similar amount from taxation opportunities to what it loses from having to pay to enforce prohibition. Converted to the scale of New Zealand, that suggests that around $200,000,000 in potential tax revenue from legal cannabis sales are instead funnelled into the pockets of criminal gangs.

Other studies suggest similar figures. According to Shamubeel Equab, who wrote a report commissioned by the New Zealand Drug Foundation, up to $240,000,000 could be claimed in tax annually from a regulated drug market (3).

This is supported by other calculations. The state of Colorado, with a similar population to New Zealand, sells USD2,000,000,000 worth of cannabis a year (4). If a similar amount was sold in New Zealand, that would mean that $400,000,000 of GST would be collected on it.

So, as mentioned earlier, the combined cost of all of the aspects of cannabis prohibition is at least half a billion dollars per year.

This is a lot of money for something that arguably has no benefit at all. Even if one charitably conceded that a majority of people wanted cannabis prohibition (they don't), or that cannabis prohibition prevented a significant amount of cannabis getting into the hands of young people (it doesn't), $400,000,000 is a great deal of money, especially when considered on an annual basis. It's about $150 a year for every taxpayer.

Had the Fifth National Government legalised cannabis at the start of their term in 2008, New Zealand would have already saved at least $4,000,000,000. The asset sales campaign run by the National Party raised barely more than this, and that was at the draconian cost of losing ownership of these assets forever.

It sounds incredible, but it's hard to deny the maths. If the Fifth National Government had legalised cannabis instead of selling state assets, they would have raised almost the same amount of money – without losing ownership of the assets.

Worst of all is that New Zealand is borrowing money from overseas sources to pay for the deficits that we're running in order to finance this prohibition. So not only did we not save $4,000,000,000, but we're paying interest on those billions – just to imprison our own young people for growing medicinal plants.

Cannabis prohibition should be repealed because it simply isn't worth the money. The total losses to the New Zealand economy from cannabis prohibition cannot be justified – even if it was charitably conceded that there was some benefit to prohibition. It would be much better to make cannabis legal, which would save hundreds of millions currently wasted on enforcement, as well as gathering hundreds of millions in tax revenue.

# 9

# Prohibition Harms Respect For The Law And For The Police

"Fuck the Police, comin' straight from the underground," go the lyrics. Many young Westerners can commiserate with the sentiment that the Police are not there to protect and serve them, but rather to harass and abuse them. But why should it be this way? Part of the reason is that cannabis prohibition has had a corrosive effect on respect for the law and for the Police.

In the Netherlands, the occupation of Police officer doesn't carry anywhere near the same stigma that it does among cannabis users in other Western countries. Not enforcing cannabis prohibition against the will of the people means that Police officers are seen as allies with a shared interest in the peaceful functioning of the community. Dutch people are not afraid to approach Police officers to ask for help or directions.

In other Western countries, by contrast, many young people see the Police as the enemy. It's hard to have sympathy for someone "just doing their jobs" when doing their job involves conducting a war against their own people on behalf of their paymasters in the Government. Actions taken by Police officers in arresting people for using cannabis, such as the ones described here (1) and here (2), are acts of evil in the eyes of most people, and certainly so in the eyes of cannabis users.

The first thought of many people, when they get high for the first time, is to immediately realise that they have been lied to about cannabis. It is not a substance that causes psychosis, but the contrary: it's a medicine that removes it (although it arguably causes psychosis in non-users). Cannabis users gain the ability to go over previous traumatic memories and view them with new, happier eyes. In other words, it's a healing herb.

This means that the Police are happy to carry out the task of imprisoning people for using a medicine, and for no other reason than that they were told to by their paymasters in Government. This is inherently disreputable conduct. Standing in the way of any sick person accessing their medicine is an act of evil, and if the Police willingly do this for money then it's inevitable that the populace come to disrespect them for doing so.

There are knock-on effects of this which form a positive feedback loop. Cannabis prohibition deters decent people from joining the Police, because they know that if they do join they will have to enforce an immoral law against innocent people. So the quality of the average Police officer goes down, on account of that the most moral and empathetic individuals disqualify themselves from service.

Another effect of cannabis prohibition is that people come to lose respect for the law. Many people, upon realising that cannabis is medicinal, ask themselves: if the Government is willing to pass a law as stupid and counter-productive as the prohibition of cannabis, who's to say that they put any real amount of honest thought into any of the other laws they pass?

This effect is certainly responsible for much of the hard drug use that people engage in. Many people who use cannabis and realise that the law against it is illegitimate come to think that laws against other drugs must also be illegitimate. This leads to them experimenting with those other drugs out of general disdain for the law. When those people discover that the other drugs are usually much less kind than cannabis, it's too late.

This process needs not stop there either: it can lead to disrespecting other laws, or even the concept of laws. If the Government is capable of passing a law as blatantly crooked and immoral as cannabis prohibition, why assume that any of their other laws are based on reason and logic?

The major undesirable effect of losing respect for the law is that social cohesion falls. After all, the vast majority of laws exist for good reason: violating them causes human suffering. Murder, rape, theft, assault – all of these cause unnecessary misery to other human beings. Cannabis does not, so if there is a law against that, then the law can't be based on preventing suffering. It must be based on something else (such as corporate control etc.).

There are a large number of medicinal cannabis users, and they are an ever-growing number. Possibly they will continue to grow for some time yet as the medicinal qualities of cannabis become apparent to more and more people. If the Police continue to attack people for using medicinal cannabis, then the level of respect that average people have for the law and for the Police will continue to fall.

Comprehensive cannabis law reform, so that ordinary people were never persecuted for using or cultivating cannabis, is necessary so that the Police and the law can regain the respect of the public.

# 10

# The Punishment Does Not Fit The Crime

Proportional sentencing is supposed to be a fundamental tenet of our justice system. When a person causes suffering to another, they are given a proportionate amount of suffering intended to discourage repeat offences: we are told that "the punishment should fit the crime". However, the punishment for cannabis offences is not commensurate with the nature of the crime.

The maximum penalty for possession of cannabis in New Zealand is three months imprisonment, as established by Section 7 of the Misuse of Drugs Act (1). Most Kiwis can intuitively understand that this is massively disproportionate to any harm caused by the act of cannabis possession, but this law is on the books, and has been for over 40 years without being repealed.

Some might counter here with the fact that essentially no-one gets sentenced to prison for cannabis possession nowadays. This counter-argument misses two essential points.

The first is obvious: if no-one goes to prison for cannabis possession anymore, on account of that society has "moved on" and no longer considers cannabis possession a crime, then it's an obsolete law. If it's an obsolete law, then we ought to strike it from the books.

The second is that people still go to prison for cannabis cultivation, which is not any more of a crime than cannabis possession is. Brian Borland was given four years and nine months imprisonment (2) for unrepentantly growing cannabis – an incredible punishment if one considers that no-one was harmed by his actions.

Some people were outraged by the sentence given to Devonte Mulitalo, an Auckland youth worker who groomed and sexually assaulted a 12-year old girl, coercing her to perform sex acts on him. He was given ten months home detention (3). Many thought this sentence was too light, and in comparison to Borland's sentence it seems obscene.

Takaka resident Alicia Fulcher-Poole was given three and a half years in prison for killing someone while driving high on methamphetamine (4). It's incredible that reckless disregard for human life resulting in a death can receive a less severe penalty from the system than growing a medicine without permission. But this is the state of our "justice" system.

It's apparent to almost everyone that 57 months imprisonment for growing cannabis is a ludicrously disproportionate punishment, when the total suffering caused by growing cannabis is compared to the suffering caused by killing someone through reckless use of a motor vehicle. Even if one assumes the most uncharitable interpretation of Borland's motives, he didn't kill anyone.

Borland's sentence was getting up towards the maximum end of the scale, which is seven years imprisonment (5). This is a heavier sentence than the sentences that are routinely given out for killing people in motor vehicle crashes resulting from reckless or dangerous driving or being intoxicated behind the wheel.

Moreover, the effect of having a criminal record lasts longer than the sentence, and sometimes much longer. Branding someone a criminal – even if there is such as thing as the Clean Slate Act – is to consign them to a lower class of citizen, one that is precluded from many opportunities that normal people take for granted.

Even a measly cannabis possession conviction is enough to prevent someone from being allowed to enter a variety of countries, most notoriously America. Neither will it be straightforward to work as a Police officer, teacher or other Government employee. This is a heavy, heavy punishment just for being caught in possession of a medicinal flower.

This loss of travel and employment opportunity is enough to significantly lower the quality of a person's life. Getting involved with cannabis should never mean that a person is consigned to live as a lower class of citizen for the rest of their lives. This is a level of arbitrary cruelty that borders on barbarism.

Cannabis prohibition should be lifted because it's not right to have such brutal punishments for actions that do not cause suffering. It makes a mockery of the supposed proportionality of the justice system. Using the criminal justice system to deal with cannabis is an absurd over-reaction to something that doesn't harm others.

# 11

# A Criminal Record Is A Disproportionate Punishment

Cannabis possession or cultivation are currently crimes, which means that a criminal record is a common result from being arrested for a cannabis offence. Our justice system, however, is supposed to operate on the principle that "the punishment fits the crime". Getting a criminal record for anything to do with cannabis is grossly disproportionate, considering the severity of the crime.

Having a criminal record makes a person's life a lot harder. Many employers will filter out applicants with criminal records before they even begin to consider them. This is true of almost every job that requires any real responsibility. This means that a future of poverty, or at least severely limited economic opportunities, is a common consequence of getting a criminal conviction.

Of course, having a criminal record is supposed to make people's lives harder. A criminal is a person who has declared that they are unable or unwilling to abide by the rules of decent society, and it's fair that they're marked as such for the safety of other people. We're not allowed to chop people's hands off anymore, so there's no other way to clearly mark a person as a member of the criminal class other than to give them a record.

The problem is that cannabis use isn't a crime like a real crime is. Real crimes have victims. It's fair that a criminal record marks a person who has acted with gross disregard or malice towards life and towards the suffering of others. But a person who grew some medicinal cannabis plants has not shown any callousness or ill will. If anything, they should be rewarded for taking actions to alleviate human suffering in the face of discouragement from the law.

Becoming unemployable because of a criminal record is one thing if you are a murderer, rapist or fraudster. In cases like these, it's probably fair for the vast majority of employers to rule such people out from the beginning. But a person who used cannabis, even if they grew it, has not done anything to warrant being placed in the same class as those who have callously brought harm to others.

In any case, that's not where the punishment ends. Most fair people can agree that it's unnecessarily brutal for a person with a cannabis conviction to have trouble finding work for the rest of their lives, but it's also extremely hard to travel with a criminal conviction. Many countries – Canada and America among the most famous – regularly refuse to let people in if they have a criminal record, reasoning that they have failed to demonstrate sufficient good character.

These two punishments tie in with each other. Many jobs nowadays involve international travel, and this pattern looks set to continue as the world continues to globalise and integrate. This means that, in order to be able to perform an increasing number of jobs, one needs to be free to travel internationally. A person with a criminal conviction preventing them from travel is effectively disqualified from all of these jobs.

Forty years ago, when the War on Drugs was just ramping up, the sort of person who got a cannabis conviction probably wasn't likely to travel overseas anyway. But in 2019, being restricted from overseas travel for life is a heavy punishment indeed.

It's worth noting here that a criminal record also affects the wider family. An adult whose employment and travel opportunities are restricted will have trouble providing not only for themselves, but also for their families. So the children of people who grow up with cannabis convictions are also punished.

All of this constitutes obscene cruelty, especially when it is considered that cannabis is a medicine, and that most people who grow it do so to alleviate suffering.

It was once – falsely – believed that cannabis caused a lot of harm. When it was thought that cannabis was a dangerously addictive drug that destroyed peoples minds, then giving someone a criminal record for cannabis may have made some vague kind of sense. Now that we know that cannabis prohibition was built on false premises, it is apparent that giving someone a criminal record for dealing with it is unfair.

In this case, the correct thing to do is to formalise this state of affairs, and as soon as possible, by repealing cannabis prohibition. We can no longer, in good faith, argue that giving someone a criminal conviction is a punishment that fits the suffering caused by the supposed crime.

# 12

# Cannabis Is An Alternative To Booze

Alcohol is great fun – but it also has its downsides. Severe downsides. Violence, sexually transmitted diseases, mental disorders and verbal abuse: when the booze goes in, it all comes out. The downsides of alcohol are severe enough that we ought to be permitted a recreational alternative in the form of cannabis.

The downsides to widespread alcohol use are considerable. The New Zealand Police Manager's Guild Trust (1) states that "alcohol is present in about 30 percent of family violence incidents they attend," and according to the study *The Burden of Death, Disease and Disability due to Alcohol in New Zealand* (2), 3.9% of all deaths in New Zealand can be attributed to alcohol misuse.

Any Police officer, emergency nurse, heart surgeon, barman, oncologist or taxi driver could give you supporting evidence. We are doing tremendous damage to ourselves on a daily basis through widespread consumption of a drug that has a number of highly toxic side-effects. The bashings, the rapes, the bodies wrecked in traffic accidents represent a great deal of human suffering – and we're not given a recreational alternative.

Alcohol brings a great deal of joy, of course, which is why it should not be banned. The anti-depressant effects of being able to have a good time with friends is incalculable, even if one can measure the physical damage in dollars. Ultimately, we cannot say that any action that causes us to enjoy life without harming anyone else is immoral, and most alcohol use falls into that category.

However, much of it doesn't. For those of us who do not wish to participate in the weekly debauchery, violence and chlamydia-fest that is the New Zealand alcohol culture, there should be a recreational alternative.

In Amsterdam, where recreational cannabis is effectively legal and sold openly from "coffee shops", we can get a glimpse of what a cannabis-based recreational alternative to alcohol might look like. On the Rembrantplein on any sunny day, one can see a park full of people peacefully smoking cannabis, with no violence or disorder. This is not just because Dutch people are well-behaved (because Dutch people chimp out on booze much like anyone else) – it is more that non-violence goes hand-in-hand with cannabis use.

The fact is that cannabis is a relaxant and a pacifier, and it tends to make people more quiet rather than boisterous. So one of the best things about repealing cannabis prohibition is that it would give people a recreational alternative to alcohol. This means that anyone wanting to relax and unwind on the weekend wouldn't be forced to partake in the culture of a drug that was associated with violence.

Indeed, it can be observed that rates of sex and violence crimes decrease in the wake of cannabis legalisation (3). This has been observed in the American states that legalised recreational cannabis after Colorado did so in 2014. The obvious explanation for this is the vastly different effects that cannabis has on human behaviour compared to alcohol.

This is of utmost importance to those who are not compatible with alcohol, for whatever reasons. Many people know that they are not well-suited to drinking alcohol, because they tend to end up in trouble with the Police. When fully sober, many people can tell you that if they start drinking they will start fighting. But there's no recreational alternative.

Legal cannabis would allow people to have options when it came to unwinding and having a good time. If they didn't want to get messy they would be able to simply go to a cannabis cafe, and get blazed and talk some shit without the risk of violence.

Of course, the fact that cannabis is an alternative to booze is one reason why it's suppressed. It has been demonstrated previously that political parties are soaked in donations from the alcohol industry (4), and that the purpose of those donations is to incentivise the politicians to vote against cannabis law reform. In other words, alternatives to booze mean lower profits for the booze industry.

This shouldn't prevent the correct actions from being taken. Ultimately, the best option is to legalise cannabis so that there is a recreational alternative to alcohol. Those who are compatible with alcohol can drink alcohol, and those who are not have the option of using cannabis to unwind. This is much fairer and safer method of dealing with people's recreational needs than by forcing them all to drink booze.

# 13

# Other Acceptable Drugs
# Are More Harmful

The standard prohibitionist argument is that cannabis is too harmful to be allowed and this is why it has been made illegal. This extreme level of harm is ostensibly the reason why criminal penalties are applied to its possession and cultivation. However, this argument is no less hypocritical and dishonest than all the others.

There's no doubt that alcohol and tobacco are more harmful than cannabis. In New Zealand, alcohol is believed to kill between 600 and 800 people every year (1), mostly from cancer, heart failure and liver failure. This is a horrendeous body count by any standard, even higher than the suicide count and the road toll.

The butcher's bill for tobacco is even worse – this is believed to kill 5,000 people in New Zealand every year (2). 1 in every 1,000 Kiwis killed every year by one legal drug can only really be described as carnage. It's orders of magnitude more destructive than cannabis, which is not conclusively known to kill anyone.

This argument for cannabis law reform is therefore very simple. If alcohol and tobacco do not meet the threshold for causing sufficient harm to be banned, then neither does cannabis. Put another way, if either alcohol or tobacco are acceptable when judged by balance of harm, then so is cannabis.

Others will respond that there's no reason to add yet another harmful drug to what's already available.

As mentioned elsewhere, this argument is ignorant of human psychology. People who want to get high will use whatever is available to them. There are no perfectly sober people enjoying their lives right now who are at risk of becoming a cannabis addict after one puff. There are, however, a lot of hard-core alcohol, tobacco and pharmaceutical users who would switch to using cannabis instead if it were available.

In much the same way that voting in an election means supporting one evil for the sake of defying a greater evil, many people use cannabis instead of a drug that is more harmful. In other words, cannabis can serve as a substitute for alcohol. This point has been argued at length elsewhere (see Chapter 12), but it's important enough to be worth bringing up again here.

If you could reduce New Zealand's alcohol consumption by a quarter, you should also reduce its death toll by 150-200 every year. A proportion of people would use cannabis instead of alcohol if they were given the opportunity, so if legal cannabis would reduce the alcohol intake then it would save lives.

Even if a third of those who gave up alcohol for cannabis died from complications related to cannabis use (a ridiculous idea if one realises that legalisation will mean vaping instead of smoking), this would still represent a saving of 100 or so lives every year. So if other drugs are both more harmful than cannabis and legal, then it makes sense that cannabis should also be legal, because then some people could switch to it.

Some will respond that alcohol and tobacco are "part of our culture". Well, we cannabis users would respond that cannabis is part of our culture. Certainly no-one asked us what our culture was, and if they had asked, many of us would have told them that we prefer to use cannabis. The people who made the decision are in the pockets of big alcohol manufacturers – they're not objective judges.

For those of us who are part of the cannabis culture, using cannabis simply fills the same niche as those who recreationally use alcohol or tobacco. We know that it's slightly physically harmful and can be mentally harmful if misused. Everyone knows this. It's just that we believe the social, emotional and psychological benefits of recreational cannabis use outweigh the minor harms.

Yet others will argue that "the horse has bolted" when it comes to alcohol and tobacco. These drugs are so widespread that they are now impossible to prohibit.

However, the same is true of cannabis. Cannabis is easier to manufacture than alcohol, and getting hold of seeds is barely more difficult than getting hold of seeds for any other plant. Cannabis is everywhere in New Zealand, and plenty of people are willing to help others get seeds (or even clones) simply to defy the Government. An entire underground culture dedicated to its survival and propagation exists.

If it's too late to enforce alcohol prohibition, then it's too late to enforce cannabis prohibition as well.

In the end, the fact that there are drugs that are both more harmful than cannabis and legal is proof that our drug laws are not logical. Indeed, our drug laws are based more on past hysteria than any sober appraisal of the evidence. Cannabis law reform would be the first step in rewriting these laws to achieve harm minimisation.

# 14

# Prohibition Harms Minorities

Cannabis prohibition causes harm across most levels of society, but some bear the brunt more than others. In the Western World, it can be seen that cannabis prohibition has a disproportionately heavy effect on minorities, and there are multiple reasons for this. This chapter will discuss the need for cannabis law reform from an ethnic rights perspective.

The South African High Court found in a recent judgment (1) that "the criminalisation of cannabis [...] is certainly characterised by the racist footprints of a disgraceful past." In other words, the South African authorities are willing to admit that cannabis prohibition was forced on the people of South Africa out of malice.

They found that "it is general knowledge that some sections of the [Black] population have been accustomed for hundreds of years to the use of dagga, both as an intoxicant and in the belief that it has medicinal properties, and do not regard it with the same moral repugnance as do other sections of the population."

It followed from this that the prohibition of cannabis and the normalisation of alcohol was to put European values first and foremost, and this was mentioned in part of their judgement when they made recreational cannabis legal earlier this year.

Ever since Jamestown – and possibly long before then – European colonialists knew that native peoples had a great susceptibility to alcohol. The American Indians called it 'firewater' for the explosively violent behaviour it caused among their kind. Rolling a barrel of rum into an Indian village had a similar effect to rolling a barrel of gunpowder into one.

The science is like this: in Europe, most of the people who could not handle alcohol had been wiped out of the gene pool over thousands of years of exposure. Many who chimped out when drunk got killed or put in prison, and thereby failed to reproduce. Consequently, Europeans (much like Middle Easterners) do not lose self-control when drunk at the same rate as peoples who have not had that historical exposure.

The people who conquered the New World did not understand the genetics behind this, but they were well aware of the destabilising effect that alcohol had on native communities. So they passed laws, such as cannabis prohibition, that forbade any alternative to alcohol. This forced the natives away from cannabis and forced them towards drugs that would destroy them.

Laws prohibiting alternatives to alcohol are extremely prejudiced in favour of European people and people of European descent. In terms of the damage it can do to people who don't have a genetic resistance to it, alcohol is almost a bioweapon, and passing laws that prohibit recreational alternatives to it could rightly be seen as acts of genetic warfare against non-European populations.

In New Zealand, Maori leaders like to talk about economic reparations and the damage done by colonisation. But seldom do they talk about the damage done to Maoris by cannabis prohibition.

Maoris have no cultural tradition of alcohol drinking. Unlike Europeans, Polynesians have only been exposed to alcohol for a few centuries. This means that they have not had time to evolve a resistance to the substance, and neither have they had time to make alcohol part of their culture. Alcohol is a foreign substance to the New World, and it's foreign to the natives here.

As anyone with a clue knows, Maoris love cannabis. Not only do you frequently see them smoking weed at parties, but it's common to see them in the street wearing Bob Marley t-shirts or with the red-yellow-green of reggae culture somewhere in their clothing. Their love of cannabis is unrepentant – in other words, it's part of the culture.

The reason for this is simple: not only is cannabis great fun, but Maoris are also aware of the destabilising effect that alcohol has on native communities, and have found that their social recreational drug needs can be met just as well by cannabis as by alcohol (in most cases). Given an even playing field, it's better to smoke cannabis because it leads to much fewer problems, in particular much less violence.

However, although this behaviour is fair, rational and reasonable, it's prohibited. There are hundreds of Maoris in prison right now for cannabis offences, even though the prohibition of cannabis has nothing to do with their culture and is something that was forced on them by (some) white people.

It follows, then, that anyone who is truly interested in racial justice in the West must also be in favour of cannabis law reform. This will not only give minorities an alternative to alcohol, instead of having alcohol culture forced on them, but it will remove one possible source of discrimination against those minorities by taking the issue away from Police discretion.

# 15

# It's Easier To Stop Using Cannabis If It's Legal

Many people take an overly simplistic approach to cannabis law reform and assume that cannabis prohibition leads to less use and less desire to use. In truth, much like the fact that people don't use more cannabis in places where it is legal (1), cannabis prohibition doesn't even help addicts. It would be easier for people to stop using cannabis if it was legal.

The logic appears to be that making cannabis illegal will make people decide to stop using it. If it's not possible to openly grow and sell cannabis, some people reason, then it won't be as easy for a person to maintain a cannabis habit, and therefore people will be incentivised to quit.

Many people who support this theory seem to assume that cannabis users, many of who are using the substance for medicinal reasons, will just sit and mope for a while and then go and do something more productive. Not only does this ignore the obvious fact that it's easy to get hold of cannabis pretty much anywhere in New Zealand, it also ignores human psychology.

The reality is, thanks to the wonders of something called variable interval reinforcement (2), prohibiting cannabis actually makes addicted cannabis users more addicted. Under prohibition, because a person can never be sure if they can maintain a supply, they come to cherish cannabis a lot more when they do get it. So when they do use it, the reinforcing effect is much more powerful.

There are two major reasons why legal cannabis would make it easier for those who are cannabis addicts to quit.

It might not be easy for the average educated, middle-class person to appreciate, but not everyone trusts their doctor or mental health worker. Just because the average Normie considers their doctor to be an intimate confidante doesn't mean that the average cannabis user feels the same way.

Attitudes have changed sharply compared to some decades ago, but there's still a lot of distrust on the part of many cannabis users towards health professionals. So if they are honestly advised to quit cannabis for good reasons, they are less likely to pay heed, because they can't be sure if the advice is coming from a place of honesty or is a formality due to the law.

It's not easy for a doctor to say that cannabis would be beneficial if it is not legal. For one thing, they don't want to get a reputation for being the local cannabis doctor. For another thing, there are potential professional consequences. None of them want to have to explain to a professional board why they recommended an illegal drug to a patient.

If cannabis were legal, it would be possible to trust your doctor if they said that you wouldn't benefit from using medicinal cannabis. As it is, if your doctor does not recommend medicinal cannabis, it's impossible to know if they say this because they believe cannabis would be harmful, or if they believe cannabis would be beneficial but are afraid of potential professional or legal consequences for saying so.

The second major reason is that legal cannabis would make it easier for a user, once they accepted that they were addicted, to taper down their use with the intent of stopping.

This relates to the reinforcement schedules referenced above. In the same way that it's better to use variable interval reinforcement to strengthen a response, it's better to use fixed interval reinforcement (3) to weaken one. This is because it leads to a gradual weakening of the craving, rather than taking it full force and risking a relapse.

Anyone who has tried to suddenly stop using tobacco or alcohol knows how difficult it is to just make a clean break with it. In most cases, if there is not an immediate threat of death, a person will be advised by their doctor not to quit cold turkey but rather to taper down over a few weeks or a month. As mentioned above, this is partly to avoid relapse, but it's partly because this is less painful.

People who were interested in stopping their cannabis use could, if we had a sane system, get a prescription for a fixed amount of cannabis with a view to tapering off. They could be given a number of joints and told to smoke x for the first week, x-1 for the second week, x-2 for the third week – or whatever worked.

This would prevent the disaster scenario familiar to people who have tried to stop smoking tobacco or drinking alcohol, in which one sits there while the craving for the drug rises and rises, until one finally caves, at which point using it feels like a divine gift. As mentioned above, this variable interval reinforcement only makes it much harder to quit.

Legal cannabis would be much better for those addicted than prohibition is. It would encourage addicts to trust their doctors when they suggested that cannabis had no medicinal value for them, and it would enable those doctors (or psychologists) to provide a schedule of decreasing fixed reinforcement that would allow for a relatively painless transition to sobriety.

# 16

# Prohibition Harms
# The Youth

One of the most common reasons given for cannabis prohibition is thinking of the children. Apparently it follows logically from thinking of the children that the criminal justice system has to imprison cannabis users. The reality is that cannabis prohibition actually harms the youth more than it helps them.

To begin with, we can see that the prevalence of youth cannabis use is much greater in New Zealand, where cannabis is illegal, than in the Netherlands, where it is legal (1). This is true whether prevalence is measured on a lifetime or a past year basis.

This one fact alone blows out of the water the prohibitionist contention that the rate of youth cannabis use would inevitably go up if the substance was legalised. It shows that having legal cannabis doesn't necessarily mean that young people use it more, despite the lazy assumption that making a substance illegal inevitably means that there is less of it available.

The lawmakers who came up with the cannabis laws are so old and so out of touch that they have forgotten how young people think.

A report in the *Scientific American* (2) referenced a study showing that teen cannabis use actually fell in Colorado after recreational sale to adults was legalised. The *Denver Post* ran a similar report (3), referencing a different study that also concluded that teen cannabis use did not increase after repeal of prohibition.

There are a variety of plausible reasons why this might be the case. The first is that cannabis use is already at saturation point among the young – anyone who really wants it can get it, without too much difficulty. Therefore, making it legal will not make it available to people who could not otherwise get it.

A second reason is that licensed, legal cannabis sellers, being no less reputable and professional than licensed alcohol sellers, will check teenagers for ID before making sales, and will turn away anyone who can't prove that they're of legal age to buy cannabis. This does not happen at tinny houses, for obvious reasons. Therefore, if a person is truly interested in preventing cannabis sales being made to teenagers, legal cannabis is better than the black market model.

If cannabis prohibition does not even help to keep cannabis out of the hands of young people, then there is no justification to continue with the policy. After all, getting arrested and tried by the criminal justice system does considerable harm to people, especially when they are guilty of nothing but using a medicine. It is traumatic to be arrested and hauled before a judge like a criminal.

Even if we assume, for argument's sake, that it's worthwhile to keep cannabis out of the hands of young people (for mental health reasons or similar), if a criminal deterrent fails to achieve this then keeping one in place is only maximising harm for no good reason. Protecting the youth would therefore demand some kind of cannabis law reform, in order to protect them from the criminal justice system.

A final argument is that alcohol is the drug of the Baby Boomers, not of young people. Young people should not be limited to alcohol when it comes to recreational drugs, because alcohol does not occupy a central and exclusive part of our culture. For the young people of the West of 2019, cannabis is just as much a legitimate choice of recreational and social drug as alcohol.

The best approach towards the youth would be honesty. Many members of Generation X and many Millennials do not trust the Government on account of previously being lied to about cannabis. This distrust does not help young people – in fact, it harms them, by inducing them to stay away from sources of official help when those might be needed.

Cannabis law reform is a better choice for protecting the youth. This is primarily because it would take the sale of cannabis out of the hands of criminal gangs, and put it under the aegis of licensed professionals who would be aware that they could be fined and lose their license if they sold to anyone under 18 (or whatever the legal age for recreational cannabis consumption would be).

# 17

# An Elderly Perspective

The perception that old people are generally anti-cannabis is far from a myth. Although many elderly cannabis enthusiasts have plenty of friends who are pro-cannabis, statistics show a strong negative correlation between being aged 65+ and voting for the Aotearoa Legalise Cannabis Party in 2017 (1). This chapter describes what those enthusiasts already know: that there is a strong case for cannabis law reform from an elderly perspective.

The unpleasant truth about getting old is that it tends to involve a lot more healthcare than being young. Getting old is tantamount to the body crapping out. It's a miserable truth to acknowledge, but there is a strong correlation between aging and physical suffering.

Because of this elevated degree of physical suffering among the elderly, there is an elevated demand for medicines of all kinds. Everyone knows that old people are always popping pills for some ailment or other. The increased sickness and frailty that comes with aging means that elderly people are interested in all kinds of medicine and, increasingly more nowadays, in cannabis.

One of the areas in which cannabis has shown the most promise for the elderly is an alternative to opiates for the sake of pain relief, particularly in the case of cancer and terminal illness. An article in the *European Journal of Internal Medicine* (2) describes how cannabis was found to be a safe and effective medicine for the elderly population in this way. Its greatest benefit seems to be found in replacing opiates and thereby avoiding their profound and unpleasant side-effects.

Cannabis has also shown promise in treating a number of conditions that are much more likely to afflict the elderly, such as Parkinson's (3), insomnia (4), some forms of chronic pain (5), age-related cognitive decline (6) and hypertension (7). This is only a small sample – cannabis has also shown promise in treating entire classes of illnesses, in particular inflammatory ones.

Despite the attempts by prohibitionist interests to equate cannabis with more harmful substances such as tobacco, the fact is that a vast range of medicinal uses for cannabis are already known. It's very possible, given the evidence thus far, that further research into cannabis will uncover new ways to alleviate the suffering of the world's elderly.

Some will make the argument that all of this evidence is in favour of medicinal cannabis only, which is an entirely separate issue to recreational cannabis. But just because the elderly have plenty of reason to support medicinal cannabis doesn't mean that they have reason to oppose wider cannabis law reform.

It has been discovered in Canada that freeing up restrictions on "recreational" cannabis encourages doctors to write prescriptions for medicinal cannabis (8). When recreational cannabis is illegal, this normalises the idea that cannabis itself is harmful, and discourages doctors from writing prescriptions for medicinal cannabis. Therefore, the two issues are inseparable.

The fact is, as Edward Bernays might have told us, that the amount of research that gets done into cannabis medicine for the elderly is a direct function of the degree of positive sentiment towards cannabis that exists in the wider society. The more people in general feel that cannabis is helpful and not harmful, the more likely someone is to suggest to research its medicinal qualities, or to agree to fund such research.

So the elderly everywhere have an interest in liberalising restrictions around cannabis, because this will lead to doctors taking an interest in the application of the plant to alleviating the suffering of conditions that afflict the elderly.

All of these things add up to there being good personal reasons for elderly people to support cannabis law reform.

After all, the elderly overseas support cannabis law reform – it has been noted that many of the beneficiaries of cannabis law reform have been elderly. The fastest-growing group of cannabis users in legal jurisdictions are the over-65s (9). The article linked here, from the *Journal of Gerontology and Geriatric Medicine*, states "marijuana use seems normalized among the older populations as more of those who ever used marijuana age."

The fact that many elderly are against cannabis law reform, despite being the major beneficiaries of it, is not a contradiction. Those generations were the ones exposed to a viciously anti-cannabis mentality that was not above telling lies to demonise the plant. Because of this normalisation of the idea that cannabis is harmful, it's understandable that someone raised in this era might still believe so.

However, there remains a moral imperative to look honestly at the evidence for and against cannabis before making a decision to support its prohibition. This ties in with one final thing the elderly might like to consider: the question of goodwill. This is a question of what kind of legacy they want to leave for those who come after them.

The Police are unlikely to arrest old people for cannabis offences (although they do). They are much more likely to go after the grandchildren of those old people. When the grandchildren of old people get criminal convictions for using cannabis, they have to live with those for the rest of their lives, and (as argued in Chapter 11) the effects of a criminal record are disproportionate to the suffering caused by cannabis offences.

The elderly don't win from their offspring getting criminal records.

Ultimately, the elderly might like to think about cannabis law reform, not just for their sake but for their children and grandchildren. It will be those generations who will be looking after them in the old folks' homes, and many of the nurses who work there would like to have access to cannabis to unwind after a day of work. The smart thing to do might be to stay on their side.

# 18

# Cannabis Meets The Industrial Needs Of This Century

For better or worse, humans will always use drugs to help them cope with the demands placed on them by the daily need to survive. Whether to help focus, relax, kill pain or to see beyond, people will always find reasons to want to change their perceptions so as to best meet the demands placed on them. Cannabis law reform is superior to prohibition when it comes to meeting the industrial demands of our time.

During the Age of Exploration, the drug of choice was alcohol, usually rum in particular. Rum had a high alcohol volume and was easy to keep. For men spending months or years at sea in ships, rum offered the best bang for the buck. Wherever European sailors took harbour, the rum trade followed. Names like Port Royal and Kororareka became synonymous with drunken debauchery and destruction.

In the first half of the 20th century, we ran out of places to explore and started killing each other over what had already been discovered. This required a combination of drugs, and these – because of the necessities of wartime – were indulged in without shame or sanction. Alcohol was still used to a great extent, particularly for its ability to give men the courage to face enemy gunfire, but use of opiates and tobacco were also widespread, the former on account of its use in physical medicine and the latter on account of its use in psychological medicine.

In the second half of the 20th century, the focus shifted from killing the enemies of liberal capitalism to making money. During this time, people were mostly tasked with social office work. This required more tobacco, but also more caffeine. It was here when the idea of becoming "caffeinated" to deal with the pressures of the day arose. The idea was that the buzz from caffeine would make the inherently safe and secure office jobs less boring.

So far this century, a lot of this work has become antisocial. This has necessitated the rise of caffeine, in order to concentrate for longer periods of time despite low levels of stimulation. This rise has been aided by the increasing unfashionability of tobacco smoking, so that caffeine has now become the go-to drug for anyone wanting more yang energy.

It's not easy to forecast the precise details of the future, but if one understands the basics of a subject it's possible to forecast general trends. What seems apparent, in the case of the Western World, is that cannabis has come to replace some of these other drugs as the one that best helps people meet the demands of the workplace, and will continue to do so.

Because of automation, it's no longer as important for the workforce to be attentive, alert and focused. This is still important for certain roles, but those roles have become an ever-diminishing proportion of the workplace. The roles that have become an ever-increasing proportion of the workplace are those in the creative professions, and the demands of these roles are compatible with cannabis use.

It's widely known and accepted that much of the world's production of quality music is made by people on drugs, and this is true to a lesser extent of literature as well. Cannabis (especially cannabis sativa) helps with the process of creativity by breaking down old conditioned pathways of thought and replacing them with novel ideas. This has made it a favourite substance of people in many creative occupations – not just music and writing but also design, cuisine, hospitality and programming.

In order to meet these industrial needs, we will not only need to legalise cannabis, but to go further. At a minimum, cannabis will need to become legal so that people who need to use it for the sake of their work can do so. For the sake of creative occupations, it will need to be gently encouraged in the workplace in the same way that coffee is encouraged in offices, and tobacco is encouraged in factories, already now.

The world is changing faster and faster, and as a result of this people find themselves confronted with original situations ever more frequently. These original situations demand original ways of thinking. The desirable qualities for employees of the future will be flexibility, originality and breadth of thought, instead of the obsessive focus and repetition that has characterised the workplaces of the past. These qualities are well enhanced by cannabis, which makes it a good choice for the workplace of the future.

# 19

# Prohibition Funds Crime

Other chapters here have mentioned that cannabis prohibition doesn't mean the cannabis market goes away: it just means that it goes onto the black market. There are several deleterious aspects to this, each worthy of separate discussion. This chapter will look at the role cannabis prohibition plays in funding crime.

The logic is that, by prohibiting cannabis and by attacking cannabis users through the justice system, it becomes possible to prevent cannabis profits from steadily flowing into the hands of criminals, which would prevent them from being able to fund further enterprises. So criminal activity, and thereby the suffering of the citizenry, can be pre-empted by attacking cannabis users and growers.

As we saw with alcohol, the attempt to prohibit a substance just makes everything about it worse. Alcohol prohibition infamously led to the rise of an entire class of gangsters and bootleggers, the most well-known being Al Capone. Because the substance couldn't be sold lawfully, it was sold on the black market, and the criminal enterprises who made the profits were happy to use that money to find other ventures.

In Capone's time, much of the black market money from alcohol sales was used to buy firearms, which were then used in the commission of robberies and contract killings. Alcohol prohibition ensured a constant flow of money into the coffers of criminal gangs, and this financed further ventures. Consequently, those criminal enterprises flourished.

We don't have alcohol prohibition any more, but cannabis prohibition has done a fine job of filling that gap.

The *New Zealand Drug Harm Index 2016* (1) stated that "Over $70 million in funding for other criminal activities is provided each year from drug trafficking. The majority of this (nearly 90%) is generated from the sale of cannabinoids." Another way to write this is to say: Cannabis prohibition puts about $60 million into the pockets of criminal gangs every single year, in New Zealand alone.

This money then finances all the murders, robberies and methamphetamine production that the rest of us have to suffer from. The Police are not wrong when they say that illegal cannabis sales fund further crime – they're just wrong when they say that the solution is to crack down on it. It's the cracking down on cannabis that makes it valuable, and this attracts the desperate, greedy and short-sighted.

If a criminal wants to fund the purchase of a large amount of precursors to methamphetamine, they might find themselves in need of a few thousand dollars. This is a similar amount of money to what they could make in one cannabis grow under a 600 Watt light, after about three months of growing. Because anyone with a real criminal network knows someone with cannabis clones (or at least seeds), just about anyone inclined to set up a meth operation can also get a cannabis grow started.

Moreover, cannabis prohibition makes it possible to cut up a pound of cannabis into $50 bags and sell them piecemeal. A criminal can do this themselves, or they can get gang underlings to do it – after all, $50 is within the reach of even high schoolers. This makes it possible for criminal enterprises to draw more and more people in.

Under a regime of legal cannabis, such things would not be possible, or would at least be strongly disincentivised. For one thing, cannabis prices are much lower in places where it is legal, and this removes most of the incentive to get involved in selling it. A second factor is that the vast majority of people prefer not to deal with criminals if they can get the same goods from a white market vendor.

So cannabis prohibition makes it possible for a variety of criminal enterprises to get funding, when they may not have been able to get off the ground without their backers' ability to sell cannabis on the black market. A lot of this criminal activity only exists because the law makes it possible. Wherever you have an economic niche, white market or black, someone will step into it.

The common counter-argument that, if cannabis was made legal, gangs would just sell hard drugs, turns out to be the opposite of the truth. The scenario we're given is that criminals will sell drugs anyway, so it's better for them to sell cannabis to our children than methamphetamine. The assumption seems to be that criminals choose to sell cannabis in preference to methamphetamine etc. out of kindness.

Leaving aside all the other ways in which this argument is wrong, it takes a certain amount of start-up capital to be able to get in on the market for hard drugs, because it's necessary to deal with major players. Cooking up a batch of meth costs money that must be invested up front, and even buying precursors usually requires a five-figure sum of cash on account of that people dealing in such are disinclined to make petty deals. Cannabis law reform would make those five figures harder for criminals to come by.

Cannabis prohibition should be repealed so as to take a major source of funding away from criminal gangs. Without black market cannabis, a number of criminal enterprises and schemes would not be able to get off the ground, which would keep our communities safer than cannabis prohibition can.

# 20

# It Doesn't Matter That Awful People Support Cannabis Law Reform

Some people – whether they're honest about it or not – don't support cannabis law reform because of the sort of person who does support it. Because many unpleasant and dangerous people think that cannabis prohibition is a bad idea, some others have gone as far as to conclude that it must really be a good idea. In reality, it doesn't matter that awful people support cannabis law reform.

Indeed, demographic analysis shows that the sort of person who supports cannabis law reform isn't the same sort of person who is doing the best. According to Dan McGlashan's *Understanding New Zealand* (1), the correlation between voting for the Aotearoa Legalise Cannabis Party in 2017 and net personal income was -0.48, meaning that ALCP supporters were among the poorest in the nation, about as poor as National voters are wealthy.

Voting ALCP in 2017 had a correlation of 0.66 with being a solo parent, 0.68 with having no formal academic qualifications, 0.79 with being on the invalid's benefit, 0.82 with being on the unemployment benefit and a whopping 0.89 with being a regular tobacco smoker. This suggests that being a cannabis supporter is correlated with just about every measure of low social standing.

Clearly, cannabis isn't a drug for people who are doing well in life. Fundamentally, cannabis is a medicine, and therefore it appeals primarily to people who are sick in some way. This is obvious from the strong correlation between voting ALCP and being on the invalid's benefit, because many of those people have discovered cannabis in their desperation. It's not surprising, then, that its supporters are generally people who aren't doing well.

None of that matters when it comes to determining the fairness of cannabis law reform.

Many people don't like to use objective, intellectual reasoning when they make decisions. As was understood by Edward Bernays (2), people often rely on the consensus opinion of the herd when they choose what car to buy, or what political party to vote for. More specifically, they rely on the consensus opinion of their peer group.

People who are in this category, and whose peer group are prejudiced against cannabis users, tend to be prejudiced against cannabis as well. Their reasoning follows the logic that, because the sort of person who supports cannabis has a low social standing, they can't have devoted any real honest thought to the issue. However, this entire argument is based on a kind of snobbery. It's little more than looking down one's nose at another person.

In fact, it's a classic example of an ad hominem fallacy (3). Just because an argument for cannabis law reform comes from a person who isn't a highly upstanding member of the community doesn't mean that the argument is false in any way. The logical validity of the argument for cannabis law reform has no relation to the social standing of the people promoting it.

Variations of the ad hominem fallacy have been used to oppose most other kinds of reform. Women's suffrage was opposed by those who characterised its supporters as spinsters and shrews. Homosexual law reform was opposed by those who characterised its supporters as AIDS-riddled degenerates. In more recent times, capital gains tax reform has been opposed by those who characterise it as expropriation and its supporters as Communists.

It's also a circular argument to say that cannabis should be prohibited because criminals use cannabis. If cannabis is illegal, then of course only criminals are going to use it. So a person cannot then turn around and argue that, because only criminals use it, this is justification for keeping it illegal.

People who use this argument tend to portray cannabis users, and cannabis law reform proponents, as brutally immoral degenerates. Dealing cannabis is viewed not as bravely supplying a medicine in the face of a tyrannical political system, but as maliciously destroying other people's brains for life. Cannabis dealers are equated to child molesters in terms of the suffering they bring.

Even if this absurd caricature was true, it wouldn't matter. In much the same way that neo-Nazis have a fair point when they talk about the effect of mass immigration on social cohesion, and in the same way that ecofascists have a fair point when they talk about the effect of vehicle exhaust pollution on the world's ecosystems, all those members of society's underclass who support cannabis law reform have a fair argument to make.

Although it's true that the strongest support for cannabis law reform comes from society's underclass, individuals within that underclass aren't necessarily there because they are evil or immoral. Most of the people who use cannabis are doing badly because they are ill, either physically or mentally – cannabis is ultimately a medicine, before it is anything else.

So just because a person is poor, or a criminal, doesn't mean that their arguments in favour of cannabis law reform can be dismissed. To the contrary – it is often people like this who are at the front lines of the War on Drugs, and understand and accounting for their experiences is crucial if we are to set the world to peace and order.

# 21

# Law Reform Is Not
# A 'Slippery Slope'

The case for cannabis prohibition is essentially based on fear, in particular fear of the unknown. Prohibitionists and other doommongers like to give the impression that cannabis law reform is a "slippery slope" to widespread social decay. This chapter argues that cannabis law reform will not be a slippery slope to selling heroin to schoolchildren, or anything like it.

The slippery slope argument is used so often that it has become a recognised logical fallacy (1). In short, this logical fallacy is when a person argues that a certain action must not be allowed, because if it is allowed, it will lead to worse actions also becoming allowed. To prevent those worse actions from coming to pass, we should keep the status quo, because to make even a small change is to step onto a slippery slope that will inevitably lead to disaster.

When we wanted to make it illegal to hit your children, we were told it was a slippery slope to those children beating up their parents. When we wanted to legalise prostitution, we were told it was a slippery slope to Weimar Republic-style child prostitution on the main streets. When we wanted to introduce a capital gains tax, we were told it was a slippery slope to the Government confiscating properties from those it deemed too wealthy.

None of these feared outcomes occurred, which is why the slippery slope fallacy is a recognised fallacy.

The slippery slope fallacy is made almost every time someone tries to change any law. So it's not a surprise that it also gets wheeled out in response to proposals for cannabis law reform. The problem is that we've had cannabis prohibition for so long now that almost no-one can remember life from before it was brought in, so we've forgotten that prohibition has done more damage than legal cannabis ever could.

The old form of this argument was that cannabis use is a slippery slope to heroin use, and therefore we have to keep cannabis illegal to protect people from getting sucked into heroin, because they're all some form of "dope". Nowadays, almost everyone knows that the sort of people who use cannabis have very little in common with those who use heroin, and don't generally move in the same circles.

Cannabis prohibitionists warn us breathlessly that liberalising the cannabis laws will lead to "THC-laced confectionery" being sold to schoolchildren. The New Zealand media has shown images of gummy bears that are purported to contain 30% or more THC, with the implication that a small child might gulp down a couple of dozen of them thinking they're sweets. Ignoring the fact that eating two dozen cannabis-infused gummy bears would still be safer than eating two dozen paracetamol, the argument fails for at least two major reasons.

For one thing, most of the arguments about the relative absence of harm caused by cannabis don't apply to other drugs. It's fair and reasonable to argue that cannabis causes less harm than alcohol; it's neither fair nor reasonable to make the same argument of crystal methamphetamine. Neither has anyone ever argued that heroin or methamphetamine was a spiritual sacrament.

Where those arguments do apply, then it's fair enough to consider them on their own merits. The War on Cannabis is, indeed, one front in the wider War on Drugs, and just because the case for drug law reform is the most obvious in the case of cannabis doesn't mean it doesn't exist in the case of other drugs. It happens to also be true that the law against psychedelics is as ridiculous as the cannabis one, if not more so.

The other major reason is that we are entirely free to recriminalise cannabis, should we reform the current laws and then decide the change isn't working. The people who have looked at the evidence and the previous experience of places that have relaxed their cannabis laws almost all believe that this won't happen, but it might. If we do decide that cannabis law reform doesn't work, we will be free to change it back.

The argument that legalising cannabis would be a slippery slope to various kinds of social decay is not valid. Cannabis prohibition is not, and never was, a wise move – prohibition is itself the experimental condition. In any case, relaxing the law is not a move into permissiveness but finally having the courage to correct an error that was made generations ago.

# 22

# Cannabis Is A Religious And Spiritual Sacrament

We are supposed to have freedom of religion in the West, but in practice this only applies to certain favoured religions, in particular Abrahamism and its derivatives. Other religious traditions, such as those that employ psychoactives as part of their rituals, are effectively discriminated against by the War on Drugs. This article will discuss the established tradition of cannabis use as a religious and spiritual sacrament.

The Indo-European peoples have been using cannabis as a religious and spiritual sacrament for thousands of years.

Cannabis is mentioned in Indian texts going back to 1,000 B.C. (1), primarily for its use as a medicine, but also for its purported ability to facilitate contact with the divine. There is an age-old tradition in India of weed-smoking holy men known as sadhus (2). These are ascetics who have renounced worldly wealth and pleasure, and who use cannabis to get into touch with Shiva. Among sadhus, use of cannabis is especially popular when meditating, for the moments of tranquillity and serenity that it is capable of bringing.

The Nepalese smoke it publicly and ceremonially during the festival of Maha Shivaratri (3). The enlightenment brought about from the cannabis high is said to represent the coming-to-awareness of the first guru in the world. It is said that it was at this moment that the consciousness of the first guru transcended the material and the illusion of space and time, and the cannabis high is intended to replicate this.

In ancient China, cannabis was used by holy men in healing and early magical rituals (4). Early Taoist shamans systematically experimented with the ritual use of cannabis, with some declaring that smoking it was as good as climbing into the mountains for those who were physically unable. Their traditions began with burning cannabis as incense for the sake of smoking out demons and evil spirits, and soon evolved into inhaling cannabis for the sake of drawing in good energy from God.

Cannabis was also used by the Scythians in a ritualistic form that amounts to the hot-boxing of small smoke tents (5). The participants would gather inside these tents as part of funerary rites and cast buds onto superheated rocks, causing them to burn and to fill the tent with cannabis smoke. The change in consciousness brought about by these rituals were considered to bring the participant into contact with the spirits of the dead.

From there, it spread to Germany, and from there to Britain and Scandinavia. The Vikings came to associate its aphrodisiac effects with the fertility goddess Freya, and spring festivals sometimes involved the ritual consumption of cannabis. Viking herbalists were also aware of the pain-killing properties of cannabis (6), and they appear to have cultivated it in Southern Norway since 650 A.D. Evidence suggests that at least some of this cannabis was cultivated for ritualistic and shamanic purposes (7).

Therefore, cannabis use has been part of our natural spiritual traditions for thousands of years. The state of cannabis prohibition brought about by Abrahamism is an obscenity. It is not right for us Westerners to live under cannabis prohibition, because it separates us from our natural connection to the divine, replacing it with a doctrine of women-hatred, gay-hatred, genital mutilation and ignorance.

Many modern people could tell you that cannabis use is still part of our natural spiritual traditions. It is the Western subcultures that smoke cannabis who are most likely to reject the obsession with materialism that has captured the mainstream. After all, the spiritual effect of cannabis comes from its ability to separate the user from the material. By inducing a state of physical and emotional calm, consciousness focuses instead on the spiritual. By pacifying the user's base physical desires, they can concentrate on a form of living that pays homage to God.

Rastafarians say of cannabis that "The herb is the key to new understanding of the self, the universe, and God. It is the vehicle to cosmic consciousness." Many Westerners who do not follow an organised religious tradition can likewise tell you that smoking cannabis gets you closer to God. There are millions of us who could tell you that we have had profound spiritual epiphanies from sacramental cannabis use, and that these epiphanies are worth gold.

Cannabis being illegal therefore amounts to religious discrimination. It's essentially no different to a law that makes the Bible or the Koran illegal. If cannabis use is a means by which some people get closer to God, how can it possibly be anyone else's right to say otherwise? The people who support cannabis prohibition would be appalled at the thought of Government agents going into someone's house to take their Bible away, but they do much the same thing with cannabis without a second thought.

There is a need for cannabis law reform so that religious and spiritual alternatives to Abrahamism can be explored. There is no valid reason for people to be forced to follow an Abrahamic tradition, and therefore no valid reason for the law to prohibit the spiritual sacraments of non-Abrahamic traditions. True spiritual and religious freedom requires that none of the established methods for coming closer to God are made illegal – this includes cannabis use.

# 23

# Cannabis Is A Tool
# For Personal Growth

The cannabis high can teach a person a lot about themselves that they didn't already know. It brings up a range of different emotions, and some of those emotions provide the sort of challenges that lead to healthy personal growth. As this chapter will examine, cannabis ought to be legal for its benefits as a tool for personal growth.

Personal growth can occur in a number of areas. For those who have suffered previous life trauma, it's common that personal and emotional development stalls at the stage where the trauma occurred. Heavy physical, sexual or emotional abuse can lead to impulsive, neglectful, destructive behaviour, and getting past such conditioned behaviours is not easy.

The main use of cannabis for psychotherapy might lie in its ability to induce a state of relaxation and fearlessness. In that state, it's possible to revisit earlier traumas and to reinterpret them. Traumatic events tend to leave the impression that they were more important than they really were, which can lead to them making a change to behaviour that outweighs any learning value the experience may have had.

A person may have become conditioned to react angrily or violently when confronted with a certain emotion or stimulus, when they really shouldn't. In order to correct this, psychotherapy seeks to revisit the traumatic event and recondition the patient to not react with anxiety when it comes up. This has the effect of settling the psychological tension that had existed ever since the trauma.

Cannabis is useful for its deconditioning effects – although this is also one of the reasons behind why it has been illegal. One man's psychological damage is another man's asset, and the brutal learned helplessness that people come to suffer as a result of early schooling tends to make them more amenable to instruction from their overlords in the workplace. Those overlords, therefore, do not want people to decondition themselves, especially if it also makes them free.

Probably the most effective use of cannabis, however, lies in its ability to cause the user to have original thoughts that could not have been generated by any other method. Cannabis has long been associated with creative industries and endeavours, especially music and writing. It does this by preventing repetitive thoughts from occurring, leaving mental space for ideas inspired by the environment.

There are several people whose minds are limited on account of the low range of stimuli they have encountered over the course of their lives. Many of these people were dumped in front of a screen by a parent when young and know little of the outside world or of other people. They have essentially been programmed to accept Disneyland as their reality.

People like this can bring themselves a new lease on life by using cannabis, and allowing themselves to explore vistas of the mind that were previously shut off. As users will attest, entire realms of new thought can open up when one is under the influence of cannabis: all sorts of strange, wonderful and unsettling ideas seem to arise as if from a parallel dimension that one could not perceive until just now.

Related to this, and as mentioned in Chapter 22, cannabis is a religious and spiritual sacrament. This entails that many people have used it as a tool for spiritual growth.

There is a reason why hippies are associated with terrifying insights into the nature of death, consciousness and reality as well as cannabis – they have seen beyond. Cannabis use can lead to spiritual growth in the same way that meditation does. By way of breaking one's usual patterns of paying mental attention to petty things, one frees up mental space for new and original thoughts to arise, perhaps from long-suppressed places.

On a darker level, the unpleasant and paranoid aspects of the cannabis experience can lead to personal growth in a grim, meathook sense. Many people have avoided ever really thinking about the fact that they're going to die, thanks to all the conditioned patterns that come with living an everyday life. So when a person does, perhaps for the first time ever, it's common for them to feel extremely challenged by it.

Cannabis law reform ought to happen so that cannabis can be used as a tool for personal growth. There are therapeutic, recreational and spiritual benefits that cannot be explored under prohibition.

# 24

# Quality Control

Libertarians like to complain about government regulation, claiming that it leads to stifled innovation and more expensive products. Although this is true of mature markets, regulation for emerging markets of any good or service usually keeps cowboys out of the industry. An argument for cannabis law reform is that it would maintain a certain level of quality within cannabis products.

The black market means a lot of things. It means shady characters, violence, turf wars, unbelievable amounts of bullshit and prison sentences. It also means a variable quality of product – and this has a number of adverse consequences for people's health.

Black market alcohol still regularly kills people in places like Norway (1), where legal alcohol is extremely expensive, because it doesn't have the same quality controls as the commercial product. As a result, the person making it often has little idea of how strong their product really is. Sometimes it's as strong as absinthe.

Despite the fact that legal alcohol still kills a lot of people, most people can understand the quality control argument against alcohol prohibition. Although legal cannabis would be much less likely than alcohol to kill people, there is still a quality control argument to be made for cannabis law reform. If one approaches the subject of cannabis law reform from a harm reduction point of view, then legalisation makes a lot more sense than prohibition.

When growing cannabis, there's not too much that can go wrong. It's called weed for a reason. Nevertheless, it's still possible to grow buds that have mold on them, especially because of the fact that they are often grown indoors in moist environments, or grown outdoors in places where the rainfall can't be controlled. This mold can easily lead to lung conditions if the bud containing it is smoked.

Much worse is that sometimes black market cannabis is sprayed with various substances that make it appear more sticky or provide more of a "hit". This can be anything from legal highs to fly spray. It might be hard for some people to believe that anyone selling cannabis could be so unscrupulous, but that's what people are exposed to when cannabis is on the black market. It's complete chaos.

None of these things would happen if cannabis was commercially grown, at least not any more often than you'd buy moldy bread from the supermarket. If it ever did happen, it would trigger a review of quality control procedures at the place of manufacture, and new procedures would be put in place to make sure it didn't happen again.

Quality control is not simply a matter of physical safety. The more science advances, the more we are coming to appreciate how many active cannabinoids there are in the cannabis plant, and how different amounts of various ones can have entirely different effects to others.

We're starting to learn that cannabinoids like delta-9 THC, while immensely enjoyable in the right context, are not necessarily helpful from a pain relief perspective. We're also learning that cannabinoids like CBD have a wide range of medicinal uses, but that it's difficult to gather useful scientific data about how to prescribe them (2), because it's hard to get hold of accurately calculated doses.

A regulated cannabis industry would allow for manufacturers to create products that had precise and known amounts of each ingredient cannabinoid. This would make it possible for doctors to prescribe a regular supply of the right cannabinoid at the right dose. In this context, the right dose means a dose that is strong enough to achieve the desired therapeutic effects without being so strong that it causes other problems.

Neither is quality control simply a matter of health.

Perhaps the worst examples of a lack of quality control can be found in the various ripoffs that occur on the black market. There are many elderly people who are desperate to get hold of cannabis medicine for conditions that cause them to suffer, and for who legal medicines are unsuitable. These elderly patients are then forced into the black market, and often get tricked into giving money to someone who supplies a substandard product – or even no product at all.

That vulnerable people can get ripped off to the tune of thousands of dollars by clowns who don't know how to manufacture quality cannabis products, or by criminals who are happy to supply rubbish that doesn't work, is one of the cruelest outcomes of cannabis prohibition. Some of these people are trying to find solace to deal with the pain of the last days of their lives, and cannabis prohibition leaves them exposed to the most exploitative elements of the black market.

This has been a common occurrence on various FaceBook groups, where old people are given a small amount of CBD oil as a sample and then asked to pay thousands for a low-grade oil that confers no therapeutic advantage. Because cannabis is illegal, these old people have no chance of getting justice through Police action. Of course, the scammers are fully aware of this, because prohibition is a criminal's best friend.

Cannabis should be made legal so as to make sure that the cannabis that people use, and which they are going to use regardless of the law, is of an adequate quality. This will not only avoid the occasional physical illness that comes from buying black market cannabis, but it will also decrease the suffering caused by criminal activity in the cannabis market.

# 25

# Effectiveness Of The Prisons

One of the major problems with cannabis prohibition is that it makes other parts of society function sub-optimally. In the same way that prohibition makes policing more difficult, and makes a mockery of the justice system, it also makes a mockery of the prison system. This chapter looks at the argument for cannabis law reform from the point of view of the prison system.

The prison system, in practice, serves a wide variety of objectives. Ideally speaking, however, it needs to fulfill one primary and one secondary objective. The primary objective is to keep society safe from the predations of criminals. The secondary objective is to rehabilitate those criminals so that they don't come back.

Cannabis prohibition is in direct conflict with this primary objective. The idea of keeping society safe from someone who grew a medicinal flower doesn't make any sense, because growing medicinal flowers helps people and doesn't harm them. In fact, doing so makes society more dangerous, for a number of reasons.

The most obvious harm is caused by taking a person who probably wasn't malicious (a cannabis user), and putting them in close contact with genuinely dangerous people, who are apt to teach that cannabis user how to become dangerous themselves. Prisons serve as universities of crime, because crime is the one thing that anyone in a prison can count on having in common with other people there.

There's no overall benefit to putting someone who has grown a cannabis plant in prison with people who are going to teach him how to manufacture methamphetamine, or to embezzle, or to commit other serious crimes. The end result will only be an actual criminal. From the perspective of harm reduction, it's counter-productive to take a person who wasn't harming anyone and turn them into a person who does harm people. It's madness.

Even worse is the harm done to the families of the people incarcerated for cannabis offences. The stress on the partner or parent of someone imprisoned is great, and lasts for at least the time of the sentence. Perhaps the worst of all is the damage done to the children, who, after seeing one of their family members locked up for nothing, inevitably come to see the State as their enemy.

One other consideration is that a person sentenced to prison for a cannabis offence may become embittered. Getting locked in a cage like an animal for an action that caused no harm is not the sort of thing can easily be forgiven. It's the sort of thing that a person tends to resent for the rest of their lives, making them a nastier person. Everyone loses from this.

In the context of cannabis prohibition, the concept of rehabilitation – the second major objective of the prison system – doesn't make any sense either.

The idea of rehabilitation involves convincing a criminal that their previous actions caused unwarranted suffering to innocent people, should not have been done, and should not be repeated. If a criminal can learn this, then they can be released into the community and be expected to not commit that crime again. As a result, the community becomes safer.

In the case of a cannabis offence, however, what's to rehabilitate? How can one go about "rehabilitating" a person who hasn't caused any harm to anyone? The fact is that it's all but impossible to convince a normal person that they are a criminal on account of that they used cannabis. It's impossible to appeal to the harm caused, unlike a genuine crime, because there isn't any.

Many people who are in prison for cannabis offences grew cannabis to meet other people's medicinal needs. These people are the opposite of criminals – they are heroes. Although they might not be seen as such by the "Justice" System, they are certainly heroes in the eyes of the people with medical conditions who couldn't otherwise access an effective medicine.

Every honest person knows that the cannabis laws are an example of illegitimate, unjust dictates, and therefore there's no "rehabilitating" a person who defies them. The laws make our prison system into a sham by putting non-harmful people there. This causes harm to everyone related to the cannabis user, as well as harm to the average person's faith in authority.

Legalising cannabis would return our prison system to its primary objective of keeping people free from harm. This would mean that our prisons were only populated by those willing to harm others, and not medicinal flower growers. This would not only make the prison system more effective, but also less cruel.

# 26

# Prohibition Harms Social Cohesion

Cannabis prohibition does a lot of harm to various groups within society, as other chapters here show, but it also has an effect on society as a whole. Not only does society have to pay for the cost of enforcing cannabis prohibition, but it suffers at a collective level the same harm done to individuals: as below, so above. One of the worst things about cannabis prohibition is that it harms social cohesion. Our society relies on co-operation between different groups at all levels.

One of the most important ways is the solidarity between generations. In order for the young to be willing to care for the old when the time comes, the youth have to feel some kind of solidarity with those older ones. They have to feel like those older ones managed the country in such a way as to leave them a worthy inheritance. They have to feel like the old cared about them.

As Dan McGlashan showed in *Understanding New Zealand* (1), there is a sharp distinction between young and old when it comes to support for cannabis law reform. The correlation between voting for the Aotearoa Legalise Cannabis Party in 2017 and being in the 65+ age bracket was -0.43 – not extremely strong, but strong enough to suggest that the average person in that age bracket is decidedly against cannabis law reform.

There are several reasons why a young person might feel that the generations before them had failed in their duty of stewardship, but the unwillingness to reform the cannabis laws are one of the foremost. For a young person today, the thought that the nation's elderly are sitting back on a fat pension drinking whisky and chomping painkillers, while at the same time putting you in prison for growing a medicinal flower, seems obscene.

Given these reasons, why would the young not come to see the elderly as evil? The indifference of the elderly towards the suffering caused to the young by cannabis prohibition certainly appears evil to those suffering it. As a result, their coming to hate those pushing it on them is inevitable. And by such means, society is divided and conquered.

Cannabis prohibition doesn't just divide society on the basis of age.

*Understanding New Zealand* also showed that the correlation between voting ALCP in 2017 and being New Zealand-born was 0.73, which is very strong. This is because cannabis use is an integral part of Kiwi culture – it brings Maoris and white people together as well as rugby and barbecues, and especially when it comes to younger demographics.

Because of the central role of cannabis in Kiwi culture, cannabis prohibition is something that pits New Zealand-born Kiwis against immigrants. This is a recipe for deep resentment, because this plays along a pre-existing fracture line in society. If the New Zealand-born would come to feel that it was only because of recent immigrants that they were not allowed to freely use cannabis, they could become very angry.

Neither is the damage done to social cohesion just a matter between different groups. Cannabis prohibition also destroys solidarity within groups.

There are occasions where people don't get together because the illegal nature of cannabis means that some people don't want to be associated with others. Many a party guest has been uninvited because the hosts were not sure that the guest would be comfortable with the cannabis being smoked there, or because the hosts didn't want the guest bringing cannabis to their house.

In such ways, all manner of natural social bonds have been broken because one or the other party was a cannabis user. This isn't just seen at parties but in romantic relationships and in the workplace too. If cannabis is illegal, then cannabis users will naturally not trust non-cannabis users and non-cannabis users will naturally not trust cannabis users. These divisions are needless.

As mentioned in Chapter 9, cannabis prohibition has had a severe impact on people's respect for the Police. But cannabis prohibition impacts other industries as well. Some people no longer trust their doctors because of their inability to speak honestly about the medicinal value of cannabis. Some people no longer trust journalists because of their past fearmongering and sensationalising over the issue. This loss of trust impacts social cohesion at all levels.

Worst of all, prohibition has caused some people to dislike their country and society, when that need not have been the case. This is especially true of those who have faced the wrath of the justice system.

How can a person respect a society that wants to put them in a cage for using a medicinal plant? How can a person respect the hypocrisy that sees hundreds of people kill themselves with alcohol every year, while at the same time targeting others for something much less harmful? Cannabis prohibition is such a poor idea that its enforcement has stoked massive anger and resentment.

All this anger and resentment has had an injurious effect on social cohesion. Prohibition has caused people to dislike and mistrust each other when they otherwise wouldn't have done so. This has had the total effect of making society worse. The only way to fix it is to legalise cannabis.

# 27

# Governments Shouldn't Conduct Wars Against Their Own People

The War on Drugs is a war that governments of the world fight against their own people, supposedly to protect people from the harmful effects of these substances. In the vast majority of cases, such government measures cause more harm than they prevent. Cannabis law reform is necessary because it is immoral for a government to conduct a war against their own people without their consent.

The War on Drugs was ramped up to full aggression by Richard Nixon in the late 1960s and early 1970s. Although the majority of recreational drugs were already illegal, the enforcement of them was not brutal until Nixon entered the scene. With the increase in aggressive drug law enforcement came an increase in the incarceration rate of Americans (1) – now four times higher than it was in 1972 (2), even when adjusted for the increase in population.

Nixon's former domestic policy chief, John Ehrlichman, is quoted in a *Harper* magazine interview (3) saying "We knew we couldn't make it illegal to be either against the war or black, but by getting the public to associate the hippies with marijuana and blacks with heroin, and then criminalizing both heavily, we could disrupt those communities." This quote encapsulates the entire logic of the War on Drugs.

The truth about the War on Drugs is that governments don't really fight this war against drugs, they fight them against their own people who use drugs. The War on Drugs is really a war against their own people.

In particular, the War on Drugs is a war against those the ruling classes want to destroy. As is clear from the Ehrlichman quote above, the ruling party is not representative of the people. They have their particular enemies, and in the case of the Military-Industrial Complex that profits immensely from defence contracts and from endless war, peaceniks are the enemy.

Likewise for blacks: the Prison-Industrial Complex demands a steady supply of slave workers to labour in prisons. This prison labour is immensely profitable for the prison owners, who occupy the same role as the slave plantation owners of the antebellum American South. So a draconian crackdown on drugs that were known to be used heavily by blacks had the calculated effect of drawing large numbers of them into the prison system.

The reason why the security services are divided into the Police and the Army is because the Army is for fighting wars, and the Police for keeping the peace. When the Government sets the Army onto the people, it's usually a sign that the Government is rotten to the core and probably not far from collapse. So when the Police are also fighting a war against the people on behalf of the Government, it's a very, very bad sign.

Everyone knows that the Government isn't really a protective, benevolent force. Everyone knows that Western governments are not representatives of their people, but rather of whatever corporate interests have declared themselves to have a stake in the country. The point is, this should not be accepted, and governments should never act to the detriment of their own people for the sake of corporate profits.

Conducting a War on Drugs makes it possible for the ruling classes to divide and conquer the people, by way of subjecting some of them to harsh legal punishment and not others. This is a grossly anti-democratic phenomenon, and should not be allowed.

Cannabis prohibition should be repealed because the Government should not fight a war against its own people. The War on Drugs is a war that the Government fights against the same people that the Government is supposed to represent and protect. It's time for a ceasefire.

# 28

# Prohibition Corrupts The Youth

As this book underlines at length, cannabis prohibition itself does a great amount of damage to our society. Leaving aside the fact that cannabis itself is not harmful, prohibition and the act of enforcing it causes legitimate harm by way of trauma, and usually to people who have done nothing wrong. As this chapter will examine, prohibition also does damage by corrupting the nation's youth.

The received wisdom is that cannabis corrupts the youth, by transforming good students into lazy, violent delinquents. The truth is much different. The truth is that cannabis prohibition creates the corruptive effect.

A young person who is taking note of the debate around cannabis law reform couldn't help but to draw some unsavoury conclusions about how the world works. Watching Bob McCoskrie shamelessly lie and scaremonger in the name of Jesus demonstrates clearly to any young people watching that our culture is rotten with crooks, our mainstream religion dead, our mainstream media complicit in it all. What sort of message is that?

The youth aren't stupid. They know that cannabis prohibition is bullshit. This can be seen from the strong correlation between being young and voting for the Aotearoa Legalise Cannabis Party in 2017 (1). The fact is that anti-cannabis propaganda has had a decreasing impact since the 1970s, by when enough people had experimented with it for there to be subcultures of individuals who knew that the reasons for prohibition were false.

This raises a question that few ask themselves, because of the rush to look tough on crime. What impression are we giving the youth by way of our actions around cannabis? Because the youth of New Zealand are watching their elders, and observing how some of those elders are blatantly lying about the side-effects of cannabis, and clearly trying to scaremonger the population, while ignoring the scientific evidence.

The youth also see the Police enforcing the law, despite the widespread awareness that enforcement of this law only serves to increase the suffering of the New Zealand people. This teaches them that the law is indifferent to the suffering of the people, merely something that is imposed upon them by Parliament, and the Police little better than dogs, merely following orders for the sake of a full belly.

Observing this blatant corruption in action has a hugely corrosive effect on the moral integrity of young people.

Above all this, cannabis prohibition corrupts the youth the worst in lower-class families. Because cannabis is on the black market, it's possible for someone to make a few thousand dollars in hard cash from running a clandestine grow. When a child sees their parent or uncle making money from growing cannabis, and not from working, then the idea of crime instead of work starts to become normalised.

Imagine if the alternative for at-risk children was watching their family member work on the white market as a cannabis researcher, or even as a budtender. A child is much better off seeing their parents work almost any job on the white market than something on the black one. It's much better to normalise the idea of making money from legal enterprise, but cannabis needs to be made a legal enterprise before that can happen.

Worst of all is the effect on those young people who see their older family members arrested and sometimes imprisoned for something which they can't understand is a crime. There's no way to get a young person, who is wise to the nature of propaganda and brainwashing, to believe that cannabis is evil enough to warrant such treatment. They know that the Government is committing an abuse against them.

The corruptive effect of this is immense. For such a young person, watching a member of your family go through that much suffering just over a plant normalises certain ideas about society. One of the most dangerous of these is that society is their enemy – an enemy that wants to destroy them.

Cannabis prohibition has corrupted our youth, by showing them that truth and justice have no place in the organisation of the world. The way to get ahead is to bribe politicians, scaremonger, lie and cheat. Political decisions about medicines are not made on the basis of evidence and science, and neither are they based on the imperative to end suffering.

It's impossible to tell a young person that they ought to obey the laws of a society when those laws are transparently arbitrary and ridiculous. This means that cannabis prohibition has had the effect of eroding the otherwise law-abiding nature of people.

It would be much better for the supposed adults to demonstrate honesty and fairness to the young people. This we could do by repealing cannabis prohibition, and then making a commitment to tell the truth about it at all levels of government, education and medicine.

# 29

# Prohibition Destroys Families

Cannabis prohibition is a destructive approach in many ways. Because of the need to use law enforcement officers to attack people who use cannabis, massive emotional trauma and psychological damage is the inevitable result of prohibition. As this chapter will examine, some of the worst damage is that inflicted upon families of cannabis users.

The most severe way that cannabis prohibition affects families is through law enforcement. To fully appreciate the destructive effect that prohibition has had on families, it helps to imagine the situation from the perspective of a child who has had a parent taken way on account of a cannabis offence.

The psychological literature is replete with information about the devastating effect that losing a parent, even temporarily, has on a child's mental health. It's common for children in such a situation to feel a powerful sense of neglect and loss. They don't understand why their parent has been taken away and put in a cage – after all, most adults don't understand cannabis prohibition either, so how can a child?

Cannabis prohibition means that children are deprived of bonding time with their parents, sometimes even for years, because of the need to put people in prison for violating the cannabis laws. This regularly has a devastating effect on the child's mental health – for no real benefit to anyone.

Another way that prohibition destroys families is by driving a wedge between generations. As mentioned in Chapter 28, the young are almost universally in favour of cannabis law reform. They know it's much safer than alcohol, and they've seen the carnage alcohol has caused to their parents' and grandparents' generations.

So when their parents start lecturing them about how they should avoid cannabis because it causes psychosis, and how they should drink alcohol instead because it's not a drug, the predictable response is that the children come to lose faith in their parents, and to trust them less.

The most extreme example of this is when one family member is using medicinal cannabis and living in the same house as another one. This often causes conflict when the owner of the house is afraid that the presence of cannabis will attract the Police. In cases like this, it's possible for the tension to lead to a family being pulled apart, and this can all be attributed to the law against cannabis.

It should be pointed out here that the damage done to families is worse than it seems at first glance. The sort of people who grow cannabis are frequently in precarious social situations. After all, one of the main reasons why people smoke it is to deal with the anxiety and depression that comes with being on society's fringes.

For these people, the safety net of the family is sometimes the difference between life or death. Vulnerable people generally don't have much else to rely on. Putting an adult in prison can have the effect of removing an important node from their family's social net, meaning that families have to go without income and children have to go without parents. Even more distant relatives like cousins, nephews and nieces can be affected.

It's common for the imprisonment of one parent to lead to the rest of the family having to move home or school. Breaking up these social networks, merely because a person grew a medicinal plant, is unconscionable. This suffering caused to family members of cannabis users is not justifiable.

Cannabis ought to be made legal so that families are no longer made to suffer as collateral damage. A repeal of cannabis prohibition would mean that the integrity of the family could no longer be damaged by the actions of law enforcement. This would avoid causing severe emotional damage to the children and wider family members of anyone imprisoned – a much more humane and compassionate approach than the one currently used.

# 30

# Cannabis Is Not
# A Gateway Drug

A common argument for cannabis prohibition asserts that cannabis is a gateway drug, in that using it inevitably leads people to using harder and harder drugs. The idea is that we need to keep cannabis illegal so as to keep people off the pathway that leads people onto truly destructive substances. There is a modicum of truth to the gateway effect – but not in the way it's usually presented.

The usual way that the gateway drug theory is portrayed is as follows. An individual tries cannabis for the first time, and experiences a cannabis high. This is a pleasurable sense of peace and euphoria that the user decides they want to have again. So they try cannabis again, and have a good time again. So they use it some more, and soon find that they need more and more of it to get the same level of hit.

Eventually the user is addicted to cannabis. After a while, cannabis is no longer able to do the job. At this point the drug user naturally comes to seek out harder drugs, such as methamphetamine, cocaine and heroin, in the hope of getting a chance to relive the original amazing high that cannabis gave them. For some reason, the idea that cannabis use leads to heroin use is particularly prevalent in some circles, especially among the elderly (which reveals that the genesis of the gateway drug theory is in old-fashioned superstition).

The logic is that cannabis prohibition should prevent people from getting exposed to that initial cannabis high, by way of making the substance harder to get hold of. The harder it is to get hold of, the fewer people get addicted, and so the fewer people who seek out really hard and destructive drugs. Therefore, cannabis prohibition protects people from the harmful effects of, for example, methamphetamine or heroin addiction.

The reality is that the gateway effect is a phenomenon that is caused entirely by cannabis prohibition, and which would mostly disappear if there was cannabis law reform, except for in the case of people who have a deathwish.

Many drugs are illegal. Of those, cannabis is particularly badly suited to serving as a contraband substance. It has a strong smell, is bulky and doesn't generate much raw profit if one considers how much time and expense goes into cultivating, transporting and storing it. Most other contraband substances are much easier to deal with and more profitable, especially those of the powdery kind.

For this reason, many unscrupulous drug dealers use cannabis as a kind of lure, by which customers can be induced to buy more profitable (and/or addictive) substances. It's common in New Zealand for cannabis dealers to suddenly "run out" of cannabis when a particular customer comes around, only to offer a hit of methamphetamine by way of compensation. If the customer decides that they do like it (and this is very common), the dealer is right there to sell them a point bag.

When the would-be cannabis user is then hooked on methamphetamine, they are much more profitable than they would have been if the only other option was to sell them an ounce of weed every two weeks or so. A person who is into methamphetamine is able to burn through thousands of dollars in a week. A dealer can potentially make twenty times as much money selling methamphetamine to a person than they could selling cannabis.

So the idea that cannabis is a gateway drug is untrue. There is such a thing as the gateway effect, but this only exists because of prohibition, in particular because of the opportunity that prohibition creates for drug dealers to get naive cannabis-seeking customers hooked on harder drugs. Far from being a gateway drug which leads to people recklessly doing coke, crack, meth, smack and anything else they can find in search of a buzz, cannabis has shown promise as an exit drug (1) for conditions like heroin addiction and even alcoholism.

If cannabis was legal, people who want to use it could simply go to a cannabis cafe or cannabis store, buy their sativa or indica as desired, and then go home without being exposed to methamphetamine or heroin or anything else. A clerk at a cannabis store is no more likely to offer the customers methamphetamine than a bartender would be. After all, they already have a steady and secure income through selling a legal drug to a set market, so why would they want to screw that up?

The truth is that cannabis prohibition forces people into the arms of criminals. This is the real causal origin of the gateway effect. Repealing cannabis prohibition would mean that the people who want to buy cannabis don't need to encounter criminals in order to so, and consequently never get exposed to a dealer offering to sell them a truly destructive drug.

# 31

# Legalisation Would Not Increase Rates Of Cannabis Use

A common prohibitionist double-whammy is to argue that cannabis should remain illegal because, if it were made legal, people would use it more, and because its use is harmful, legalisation would therefore lead to more harm. This chapter will not argue whether cannabis is harmful (this is done elsewhere (1)), but will simply summarise what the evidence suggests: that legalisation will not increase rates of cannabis use.

It seems intuitively obvious that making cannabis illegal lowers the rate of cannabis use. After all, the whole point of making it illegal was to make it harder to get, and if it were legal people would be able to buy it from shops.

Fair enough, but the statistics show a different story.

The truth is that cannabis cultivation is so common (believed to account for 1% of electricity consumption (2)) that pretty much anyone who wants to get hold of it can, except for times of unusually high demand. This means that the cannabis market is already saturated – and this can be demonstrated with reference to real-world examples.

The most obvious counterpoint to the argument that legalising cannabis will increase rates of use is the fact that rates of cannabis use are not higher in places where it is legal.

In the Netherlands, 8% of the adult population has used cannabis at some point in the last 12 months (3). This rate is lower than in Australia (10.6%), where cannabis is illegal, and much lower than in New Zealand (14.6%), where cannabis is also illegal. In countries such as Israel and

Ghana, the rate of cannabis use is higher still. Cannabis might not be technically legal in the Netherlands, but in practice anyone who wants to buy it from a shop can do so.

If legalising cannabis will inevitably cause rates of use to increase, how can it be possible that rates of use are lower in a place where it is legal, where getting supplied is as simple as walking into a shop? If the link between cannabis being legal and higher rates of cannabis use is so certain, we could expect to see higher usage rates in all the places where it is legal, and lower usage rates in all the places where it is illegal. In reality, no such correlation is apparent.

The truth is already known to anyone who has ever been to the Netherlands. Cannabis is easy to get hold of, yes, and the Police won't harass you for it, that's true, but the bulk of the population would rather drink alcohol anyway. Cannabis law reform didn't turn a large number of non-drug users into cannabis users – a small number of alcohol users became cannabis users, and the rest stayed the same.

The absence of a correlation between the legal status of cannabis and the rate of use within a jurisdiction is not the only place that statistics disprove the idea that legalisation will lead to more cannabis use.

A poll by the Colorado Department of Public Health found that cannabis use rates declined among teenagers (4) after legalisation, with rates of teenage use in Colorado lower than the American national average. Another study, the National Survey on Drug Use and Health, supports the idea that teenage cannabis use rates actually declined (5) after it was made legal.

In fact, the latter study suggests that teen cannabis use rates declined in the majority of states that recently made cannabis legal. It may be, as some have suggested for decades, that the Government lying about the effects of cannabis and exaggerating its dangers was what led to many young people becoming attracted to it. Had there never been an unjust law prohibiting cannabis, it's possible that the rebellious section of society would never have felt obliged to defy it.

At this point it could be countered that, even if teenage usage rates of cannabis go down, and even if this was the most important thing, adult rates of cannabis use might still increase if cannabis were legalised, and that this might lead to more harm. Leaving aside the fact that this argument has already been countered in the first part of this chapter, it doesn't even apply here.

There is little doubt that some people will replace recreational alcohol use with recreational cannabis use if it were legal to do so. Technically, this would mean that the rate of cannabis use would increase, but the rate of recreational drug use would remain the same. Moreover, the amount of harm caused by recreational drug use would decrease if some people replaced boozing with cannabis, on account of that alcohol is more harmful.

Ultimately, the argument that cannabis legalisation would lead to more suffering through increased rates of cannabis use is in error, for multiple reasons. A review of the statistical data shows that cannabis use is not higher in places where it is legal, and also that rates of teen use have declined in American states that have made it legal.

# 32

# Law Reform Would Bring Sense To Workplace Drug Testing

One of the worst things about cannabis prohibition is not that it gives people the opportunity to mistreat each other, but that it coerces them into doing so. The fact that cannabis is illegal means that people are essentially forced into taking particular measures when they come into contact with it. These measures often unfairly impact a number of people, which is another reason why the cannabis laws ought to be changed, as this chapter will examine.

Right now, in many places across the West, there is a common but extremely cruel phenomenon taking place. It is that of all of the people losing their jobs because of being forced to take a urine test at work, and having it turn out positive for cannabis.

The logic goes like this. Many jobs, in particular those involving the operation of heavy machinery, cannot be performed safely by those under the influence of drugs. This goes for not only alcohol and cannabis but for many other substances. These jobs require a sober mind, because anyone not sober could easily kill themselves, someone else, or do millions of dollars worth of damage.

Fair enough. But because it's not always possible to rely on a person to come to work sober, some insurance companies, as a condition of granting insurance, make it necessary for the company seeking insurance to perform drug tests on their employees so that they can remove the ones who are working under the influence of some drug, thereby making the workplace safer.

This is fair-ish, but where it truly crosses the line into unfairness is the fact that instead of testing for cannabis impairment, the urine tests test for the presence of certain metabolites that are present in the urine if the person has used cannabis at some point in the recent past, perhaps even 30 days ago (or more). So the urine test can only determine if you have used cannabis recently, not whether you're impaired at the time of the test.

This means that "failing a drug test" has got little to do with whether or not your ability to do your job safely was impaired. Many people who get fired for failing a drug test are not even impaired at the time the test was taken. So a lot of people are getting discriminated against, unfairly, on account of cannabis use that probably isn't even affecting their ability to perform their work duties safely.

In many cases, the employer is perfectly fine with this arrangement. Any employee who uses cannabis is more likely to be a freethinker and therefore disobedient, or more likely to demand a higher wage. A urine test that reveals both a tendency towards freethinking and evidence of having committed a crime is a perfect excuse to fire someone, but the option shouldn't be available.

If cannabis became legal, some things would change with regards to this arrangement. Of course, cannabis law reform wouldn't suddenly make it legal to go to work stoned. Every workplace would still be obliged to meet the same health and safety standards as before. The most likely difference is that it could become possible that any employer drug testing their staff was legally mandated to use swab tests to test for impairment, and not urine tests to test for the presence of metabolites indicating use within the past 30 days.

Generally employers prefer to do a urine sample because it's cheaper, but if cannabis were legal, an employee might be able to bring a case for unfair dismissal to court if they were fired for the presence of metabolites in the urine. Such a case might well rule that, if cannabis is legal, such an action constitutes unfair dismissal, and therefore the employer is obliged to use a swab test to test for impairment instead.

It could be argued that employers would actually benefit from this policy as well. In the modern workplace, finding staff is harder than before on account of the increased need for training and education. If a person wants to work, there's no reason why the fact that they smoked a bong two weeks ago should prevent them. The reality is that they're probably safer than someone who is hungover or on sleeping pills.

It would be better for everyone for the law to change so that some sanity could be restored to the issue. If cannabis were legal, than the workplace standard would be a swab test for intoxication, not a urine test for the presence of metabolites. This would mean that it was possible to make a distinction between stoned people, who shouldn't be in certain workplaces, and people who have used cannabis recently, who are no less safe than anyone else.

# 33

# Prohibition Raises Prices But Also Raises Incentive To Supply

One of the most common arguments for cannabis prohibition is a microeconomic one. The idea is that making cannabis illegal makes it more expensive, which means less people can afford to use it, which means the harmful effects of cannabis use are minimised. The logic is that people won't be able to afford to harm themselves. As this chapter will show, this argument, common though it is, is mistaken.

If one assumes that cannabis use is inherently harmful, then one appears to have a clear-cut case for reducing the amount of suffering in the world by making it illegal (that cannabis is not inherently harmful is another argument, and will not be considered here). Making it illegal means that only the black market is able to supply it, which means that the end user has to pay a risk premium (1) that takes into account the cost of Police harassment of the cannabis grower, and the inefficiencies that this harassment introduces into the growing process.

This risk premium makes cannabis more expensive, because the end user has to pay for all of the product confiscated by Police, or stolen by other criminal actors, or which was never grown because the size of the grow room was limited by the need to keep it clandestine. All of these factors serve to drive the price of cannabis up, which – according to the law of supply and demand – serves to reduce cannabis use.

The mathematics checks out. However, the core economic argument that cannabis prohibition reduces harm by disincentivising people from buying cannabis falls down, for a number of reasons.

It is true that prices fall sharply when cannabis becomes legal. The average price of an ounce in Colorado is NZD259 (2), which means that it has fallen almost by half since legalisation took place. Websites that track the price of cannabis across various American states (3) show that the price has fallen as low as NZD100 an ounce in places like Washington, where it is both legal and where the ability to supply is relatively unconstrained.

It isn't true that this fall in prices leads to more use. Surveys in Washington have found that teen rates of cannabis use remained the same (4) after cannabis legalisation. It is also noteworthy that teen rates of cannabis use in Holland are unremarkable in any sense (5). These surveys reveal that cannabis prohibition does not deter use.

In any case, the most important question to be asked about the high prices of cannabis caused by prohibition is this: who is getting all the money? In the same way that alcohol prohibition made Al Capone and his fellow Chicago gangsters rich, so too does cannabis prohibition funnel consumer wealth into the hands of the black market. This inevitably means criminal gangs, most of whom are deeply unpleasant people who are using the money to fund enterprises that genuinely do cause mass human suffering.

Once criminal gangs start getting involved in the cannabis trade, it means that there is going to be a lot more violence than if they weren't involved. The black market means fighting for drug turf, which means intimidating other members of the black market away from certain territories through violence and the threat of violence. It means murders, kidnappings, shootings, stabbings, standovers, and all manner of other low-rent behaviours that lower everyone's quality of life.

High cannabis prices incentivise all of this. The higher the cannabis prices are, the stronger the pull of the black market for cannabis on the various shady operators out there. Not only that, but the higher the stakes, the more ruthlessly people are willing to behave in order to secure a slice of the profits. No-one is going to kill anyone else over the right to sell cannabis for $75 an ounce.

So the fact is that, in the final analysis, the economic equation balances out. The higher the price of cannabis, the lower the demand, true – but the higher the price, the higher the incentive to get into the black market opportunities for cannabis. If you are a criminal, and you don't want to work, then growing some cannabis to sell to 15-year olds at $400 an ounce seems like an attractive proposition. If those 15-year olds are happy to wait until they're 18 to buy it legally at $150 an ounce, well then you're shit out of luck.

Cheap, legal cannabis would take a large sector of the black market, and render all criminal action in that sector uneconomic. This has several advantages, the foremost of which is that criminals can't make as much money out of cannabis as before and therefore do not dominate the market. Another advantage is that people will be consuming a much higher grade of cannabis once it's grown by professional horticulturalists and not gang members, and they will be able to do so more safely.

Cannabis ought to be made legal in order to disincentivise criminal actors from moving into the black market for it. Cheap, mass-produced, high-quality cannabis will take away the profit from what is currently a black market enterprise, which will have the effect of removing most of the criminal element from the cannabis trade. This will have the overall effect of reducing crime and suffering, because the criminal element causes more suffering than is prevented by cannabis being too expensive for some people to harm themselves with.

# 34

# Prohibition Is Cruel

There are a great number of differing political philosophies in the world, and they disagree on a great many matters. The closest we've been able to get to a universally agreed-upon value is that the Government ought to act to minimise human suffering. This chapter will make the argument that prohibition ought to be relaxed because it is cruel.

Cruelty is a malicious disregard for the suffering of other sentient beings. It was cruel to perform electroshock therapy on people without their consent. It is cruel not to summon medical help when one encounters a person in distress. It was cruel to not allow homosexuals to express their genuine regard for each other. Cannabis prohibition falls into the same category.

Some people will argue that not being allowed to use cannabis doesn't constitute cruelty because it's not really a big deal. There are many other things that we're not allowed to do, so what does it matter if cannabis is another one of those things?

But that's looking at it around the wrong way. People naturally live, and part of life is to explore what comes your way. People will naturally use cannabis, because others will offer it to them. Some of those people will find they really like it, perhaps even enough to use it daily. Punishing people for an act that they do naturally – especially when that act harms no-one – is an act of cruelty.

It's cruel to cage a bird, or keep a cat inside, because it's a violation of their natural instinct to be free. The natural instinct of a human being is to explore consciousness. Isn't it, then, an act of cruelty to prevent them? Preventing a human from exploring their consciousness is as unnecessarily restrictive as keeping a cat or dog in a small cage for their whole life.

Forcing people to follow arbitrary laws and dictates is cruel, because it makes those people feel like they are of less value than those imposing the rules. Putting someone in a cage where they suffer intensely from being in close physical contact with extremely dangerous people, just because they don't follow those arbitrary decrees, is beyond cruel. Yet, that is what our system does in the pursuit of enforcing cannabis prohibition.

Perhaps the worst cruelty is that done to the family members of those who are incarcerated for cannabis offences. For a family member who is relying on certain other members of their family for income or support, it seems almost egregious for the state to incarcerate those others on account of a cannabis offence.

It's unlikely that many cannabis prohibitionists would like to explain to a small child how the supposed dangers of cannabis are so great that it necessitates putting their parent in jail. They would much rather prefer that social workers and Police officers explained that to the children of parents imprisoned for cannabis offences. This cowardice exposes that cannabis prohibition is underpinned by an absence of compassion.

Some people ought to think about what sort of world they want to live in, because the compassion or cruelty of the laws under which we live have an impact on whether people act to ameliorate each other's suffering or not. The legal system, whether we like it or not, sets the standard for whether we are compassionate or harsh towards those who really crash out.

Passing a law that says a person has to go in a cage if they grow a medicinal plant sets a precedent for what the appropriate level of compassion in our society is. And it's a low one. Locking people up for using medicinal flowers shows that we are a brutal people. It shows that even if a person can provide a fair reason for using a medicinal substance, the Government can just bulldoze through and imprison them anyway.

Some of the older prohibitionists might like to consider that they themselves will soon be in need of compassion, because their bodies will continue to decline towards death. In a person's final few years, they are just as dependent on the goodwill of others as they are in their first few years. If one is old, therefore, it's to one's own benefit to normalise compassion and empathy.

Even if the argument is made that the point of the cannabis laws is to prevent suffering (by way of preventing addiction and mental illness), the reality is that there are hundreds of millions of cannabis users who are happy to tell you that their use of cannabis itself prevents suffering. It's cruel not to listen to these people, to tell them that their claims of being helped by cannabis are delusions and that they should be in a cage for their own good.

Ultimately, this argument asserts that there's enough cruelty in the world, and that we don't need any more. Cannabis should be legalised because it's cruel to punish people for using a medicinal flower that doesn't harm anyone. This would contribute to a world with less suffering in it – something that we all benefit from.

# 35

# Legalisation Will Not
# Lead To A Black Market

One of the fears of those who are against cannabis law reform is that a legal system of cannabis distribution would lead to the growth of the black market in cannabis production. Therefore, it would be better to keep cannabis illegal. This reasoning is based on at least two major errors.

The logic goes like this: it costs X amount of dollars to buy an ounce of cannabis – let's say 300. Cannabis is likely to be taxed in a manner similar to alcohol, and alcohol taxes are reasonably hefty, so let's assume at least a 20% sin tax on cannabis, plus 15% GST – this is already over $400 an ounce.

This could mean that legal cannabis will cause so much tax to be added to the cost of an ounce that black market operators will be able to undercut it. Since cannabis growing will not be cracked down on because of its new legal status, large numbers of people will be able to grow and to enter the black market at no risk.

This reasoning is false in two major ways:

The first is that is doesn't account for economies of scale. On the black market – which is currently where all cannabis is sold – producing cannabis isn't cheap. As discussed at length in Chapter 47, home cannabis grows suck up as much as 1% of the electricity production of nations such as America and New Zealand. These are incredibly inefficient compared to warehouse grows.

Moreover, cannabis sold in a legal market, from dispensaries, would not carry the risk premium (1) associated with a product sold on the black market. The risk premium is very high in the case of cannabis, because a lot of product gets intercepted by Police action before it ever gets sold, and the losses from this have to be balanced against finalised sales.

Taking both of these things into account, we can see that the production cost of legal cannabis, manufactured by the ton and distributed to pharmacies without interruption, is going to be a fraction of what it is currently. This means that it will be possible to put GST on it and a sin tax on top of that, and still sell cannabis for $200 an ounce, or less.

No black market producer could compete with this and still make enough of a profit for it to be worthwhile. So, if anything, legal cannabis would sooner wipe the black market out completely by undercutting it. This was a principle understood in Uruguay when they made cannabis legal in 2013 – they set the price of cannabis at $1 a gram (2).

The second major reason why we need not be concerned about a black market is because we have the capacity ourselves to more-or-less set the final cannabis price through taxation.

There are really two kinds of prohibition: hard prohibition and soft prohibition. What we have right now is hard prohibition, where the Police will physically smash anyone in possession of cannabis, or cultivating it. This is hard because it uses the full power of the State, and will go as far as killing a person to enforce it, or putting a person in a cage for several years. We are simply not allowed it and no correspondence will be entered into.

But making something legal, and then taxing it to the point where it's almost impossible to afford, is a kind of prohibition. The New Zealand Government is currently employing soft prohibition of tobacco, in that it has been raising the tobacco taxes every year, with the stated intent of forcing tobacco cessation through making it unaffordable. This it believes is in the greater good.

Soft prohibition shares many of the drawbacks of hard prohibition. In the case of cannabis in New Zealand, we can see that black market tobacco has made a comeback (3), to the point where trade in it is believed to cost the New Zealand Government tens of millions is lost taxes every year. So we can see that high taxes on legal cannabis is a bad idea, if the black market is to be discouraged.

If cannabis legalisation was done intelligently – which is to say that it was done with an entirely different mindset to how prohibition has been done so far – we would set the level of taxation such that the transition to a legal cannabis market was a soft transition.

In other words, we could calculate what the expected average production cost of an ounce of cannabis should be, account for profits, account for GST, and tax that total at a rate that would still allow it to beat the black market. This would achieve all major objectives at once.

Not only would cannabis law reform not lead to more cannabis being sold on the black market, but it would be the best thing to fight it. Cannabis law reform would allow legal sellers to undercut the black market through economies of scale and the removal of the risk premium, driving criminal gangs out of business.

# 36

# Cannabis Is Not Harmful

One of the most fundamental arguments for cannabis prohibition is that cannabis is harmful. Because of this harm, the argument goes, we need to make cannabis illegal. This will give people less opportunity to use cannabis and thereby have their lives destroyed. As this chapter will examine, there are at least two good reasons to oppose this argument.

First, we can see prohibition causes more harm than legal cannabis would – and over and above the harm caused by enforcing the prohibition. When a country or state introduces cannabis prohibition, they usually also introduce a number of ancillary laws that are ostensibly to fight the harm of cannabis, but which end up causing more harm.

It's apparent that burning plant matter and then inhaling the smoke is not the best thing you could do for your lungs. This is not a contentious assertion, and the vast majority of cannabis users are fully aware of it. But when people have tried to take measures to make cannabis use more safe, they find themselves being stymied by the law. In many cases, the law is intended to penalise not just cannabis use but the entire cannabis culture.

Manufacturing cannabis butter to make some brownies changes your crime, according to New Zealand law, from possession of a Class C drug to manufacture of a Class B drug. So if a person decided to make some hash brownies, they would then not only be in possession of a Class B illegal drug, but they could also be charged with manufacturing it – which carries a maximum penalty of 14 years imprisonment (1).

We are told that the schedule of increasing penalties reflects the schedule of increasing harm caused by these drugs. But the harm of cannabis does not increase 56 times (maximum penalty for cannabis prohibition is 3 months) because someone made some bud into some brownies. There's no logic to that at all – if anything, the harm is lessened by virtue of avoiding lung damage.

It's true that the psychoactive effect of hash brownies will be greater than smoked bud, but the psychological drawbacks of using cannabis have been massively overstated. The cozy consensus that using cannabis causes schizophrenia has been shattered (2) by new research suggesting that it is a genetic propensity to schizophrenia that predicts cannabis use, and not the case that cannabis use alone predicts schizophrenia.

In any case, it's possible that even cannabis bud does not cause net harm. Yes, smoking it is not great, but the smoke damage may be outweighed by the medical benefits of lower stress etc.

Likewise, the example of "drug paraphernalia" is another one in which the majority of the harm is caused by the law itself, rather than cannabis. People have been arrested for the possession of water bongs and charged with a more severe crime than mere cannabis possession – but using a water bong is more healthy than inhaling hot smoke. Despite being more healthy, possession of a bong carries a maximum penalty of a year's imprisonment in New Zealand.

The physical harms of cannabis have generally been overstated. Of course, inhaling cannabis smoke is not ideal but even this is transparently less dangerous than rugby, horse riding, skiing and downhill mountain biking. All of these activities, whose level of risk falls into the acceptable threshold, are legal. Therefore the "cannabis is so harmful it should be illegal" argument is nonsense.

Moreover, even the most ardent cannabis user doesn't smoke as many joints in a day as a tobacco user smokes cigarettes, and so the level of risk here falls into already established acceptable limits.

Another major argument when it comes to the supposed harms of cannabis is that prohibition is a bizarre response to any supposed harm caused. Let's say, for argument's sake, that cannabis is harmful – how does it make any sense to introduce more harm into a person's life, just because they used it? The idea of punishing an adult into taking responsibility is ridiculous.

The argument that cannabis should be prohibited because it is harmful is mistaken. Cannabis prohibition itself is responsible for more harm than cannabis is. If reducing harm done to human beings is a consideration when setting legal policies, then it's clear that prohibition ought to be repealed for the sake of a less punitive approach.

# 37

# It Doesn't Matter That Substance Abusers Use Cannabis

Some people are hesitant to support cannabis law reform because they don't want to make it easier for substance abusers to destroy themselves. Their fear is that legal cannabis will simply provide another substance for substance abusers to get wasted on. However well-meaning the sentiment, cannabis prohibition is not the best way to deal with those fears.

Like many of the arguments against cannabis law reform, this one is mostly based on a misconception of the psychology of cannabis users, and of substance abusers in general. It could be called the *Trainspotting* myth, because some people believe that the trajectory of cannabis use proceeds much like heroin use does in the film based on the eponymous Irvine Welsh book.

The fear is that legal cannabis will simply provide another way for degenerates to destroy themselves, and so why should the Government facilitate this? The fewer legal drugs available, the fewer easily-accessible avenues for self-destruction. Better to keep cannabis illegal to persuade people to go straight.

The sort of moraliser that makes arguments like this is generally not the same kind of person that hangs out with actual heavy substance users. As such, they don't understand the psychology of them. Almost no-one goes from living a completely clean life to misusing any drug just because they "got addicted".

The reason why people become substance addicts is usually because they have untreated mental illnesses, which leads to a much stronger sense of enjoyment from the feeling of being drunk/stoned/wasted. The more unpleasant one's thoughts, the more pleasant to escape from them. Therefore, it's not so much the drug that leads to the abuse but the way the mind and brain are wired.

There are cases where people are substance abusers, and it may be that, for some of these people, legal cannabis means that they abuse more cannabis than they would have done if it was illegal. If this means that they avoid abusing worse drugs, then this is a good thing. All things being equal, it's better for a person to use cannabis every day than to use several of the other drugs listed in the Misuse of Drugs Act.

There's no guarantee that any individual cannabis user is going to smoke cannabis until they die. Plenty of cannabis users, even heavy ones, get sick of smoking it and move on to other things. After all, although cannabis can be great fun, it can also get boring, much like alcohol and women and loud music and all the other things that people like to indulge in for a while.

So it's better for them to get their fix on a drug that they are going to survive than on one that is going to kill them. Let them get their kicks on something that's not going to do any long-term damage. It's much, much better for people to use cannabis – and to perhaps need a few weeks to come back to normal – than to use something that will permanently change their brain chemistry.

An intelligent approach to cannabis law reform would put the emphasis on harm minimisation. If a person is honestly concerned about the total damage and suffering that a substance abuser might cause themselves, then a regime of regulated, legal cannabis would lead to less harm, for a variety of reasons.

Substance abusers are much more likely to get help from mental health professionals if their substance is legal. This fact has been clearly demonstrated by the willingness of patients to talk to their doctors about their alcohol or tobacco use compared to their willingness to talk about their methamphetamine use. If a substance is illegal there is a lot of fear associated with it.

Legal cannabis would make it easier for actual substance abusers – the sort who are destroying their lives – to trust their doctors or drug counsellors. This would make them more likely to take advice to either quit, or, if necessary, to go on a treatment program such as one that tapers off cannabis.

Legal cannabis would also make it possible for accurate and honest educational campaigns to exist. Right now, there's no reason for any cannabis user to believe anything the Government says about the substance, because everyone knows they lie about it. So if the Government gave intelligent advice about protecting the lungs, it may not be heeded.

# 38

# Cannabis Does Not Cause Paranoia

A common piece of received wisdom about cannabis is that it causes paranoia. This paranoia is part of a wider suite of psychiatric problems that cannabis is erroneously blamed for – problems that justify putting people in cages to protect them from themselves. Like all the others, however, the argument that cannabis should be prohibited because it causes paranoia is invalid.

The truth is that it's prohibition that causes paranoia. Cannabis itself is medicinal, and has never caused paranoia in and of itself.

Proof for this is unnecessary for anyone who has used cannabis in the Netherlands or, more recently, in places like Colorado, Uruguay, Washington or California. Anyone who has done this can tell you that the same kind of paranoia that people sometimes get when using cannabis in New Zealand does not occur.

There are clear reasons why using cannabis creates paranoia in places like New Zealand.

The first group of reasons relate to the Police. The fact is that the Police do not make moral judgments about the laws they are enforcing. To the sort of person who becomes a Police officer, there's no difference between arresting a murderer, arresting a cannabis user or arresting someone for being a member of a race that the Government has targeted for extermination. The Police just enforce the law.

Therefore, anyone using cannabis in a place where it is illegal has every reason to be paranoid, because there's a chance that if their activity was discovered by the Police they could end up locked in a cage. It's possible to get seven years imprisonment for growing a medicinal cannabis plant in New Zealand, and even though a custodial sentence is unlikely for simple possession, the fear is reasonable.

All of the reasons within this first group have been created directly by cannabis prohibition itself. If cannabis was legal, there would be no reason to fear the Police or the "Justice" system whenever one used cannabis or had it in one's possession.

The second group of reasons relate to society. When a person uses cannabis and realises that it is nothing like what it is said to be like, it's natural to ask some very deep and dark questions about the nature of society. In particular, one comes to ask how it is that cannabis could have become illegal in the first place, given that it's clearly a medicine that has beneficial effects.

Eventually this leads to people asking some extremely difficult questions. If it was only possible to make cannabis illegal by virtue of telling an enormous amount of lies about it, what nefarious forces controlled the resources necessary to propagate all these lies? Who is really in control of this system, if they can make lies into a truth that is parrotted by Police, politicians, teachers and doctors?

And if doctors didn't even know that cannabis is medicinal despite the stacks and stacks of evidence in favour of the idea, what else don't they know? Or, even worse, if they did know that cannabis was medicinal but lied about it for sake of greater profit or for fear of Government disapproval, what else could they be lying about?

Naturally, all this sort of thinking is capable of creating intense anxiety – but it's cannabis prohibition that makes this possible. Without cannabis prohibition, none of this reasoning makes any sense, and is unlikely to be entertained. A pleasant cannabis experience will not cause a person to question the structure of society, unless that society has already told him that cannabis was the boogeyman.

In any case, many drugs can be anxiogenic if a person does not use them correctly. Caffeine can easily cause paranoia and anxiety if a person who isn't used to it takes too much, and this is considered humourous by most people, not a reason to ban coffee. If cannabis causes a person anxiety, they should either use a different strain (preferably one with more CBD) or abstain from using it altogether. Weed is not necessarily for everyone!

It is possible that cannabis can cause a kind of existential paranoia. Many people are conditioned to never think about deeper philosophical questions, and some of these people discover that the cannabis high induces them to do so. Cannabis can have a massively deconditioning effect, which is why artists use it, but this can lead to the user entertaining lines of thought that have otherwise long been suppressed.

The way to deal with this, however, is either to fix it by philosophy or to avoid using cannabis (or to try a form of cannabis with less THC in it). Life is anxiogenic in a myriad of ways, and therefore it's unreasonable to expect that the deeply contemplative mindset brought about by cannabis use should leave a person immune to paranoia. It is a similar case with most other cannabis-related anxiety.

The argument that cannabis ought to be illegal because it causes paranoia is false. The majority of paranoia brought on by cannabis use is a function of prohibition. If cannabis prohibition went away, most of the paranoia associated with it would also go away, therefore we're better off if it were legal.

# 39

# Cannabis Is Not Addictive

One of the most common arguments against cannabis is that it is an "addictive drug". People making this argument raise images of zombie-like addicts burgling houses and selling their bodies in dark alleyways for the money to finance their addiction. Leaving aside the fact that this fear-mongering is bollocks, the argument isn't even accurate.

The scientific literature warns us of the effects of cannabis withdrawal: "irritability, anxiety, decreased appetite, restlessness and sleep disturbances (1)", sleep problems (2) and "a constellation of behavioral, somatic, and mood symptoms (3)." It's clear that to stop using cannabis often means that one encounters these problems, but they soon go away. People enjoy using cannabis, but use alone does not count as addiction.

*Psychology Today* ran an article (4) that stated "The vast majority of those who use marijuana do so occasionally and exhibit no addictive symptoms — no increased tolerance, no cravings and no withdrawal. In other words, they can take it or leave it."

It's true that cannabis does not cause meaningful physical addiction. Something that's really addictive is alcohol. Withdrawals from alcohol are known to cause delirium tremens, a phenomenon known as "the DTs", which can kill the sufferer (5). If this is considered an acceptable side-effect of a recreational drug, then the physical addiction potential of cannabis is nowhere near objectionable.

The counter-argument to this is to say that cannabis can still be psychologically addictive. Psychological addiction is a kind of excessive habituation, where a person does not become medically ill but can suffer "psychological symptoms like anxiety, mood swings and depression".

At this point, another frightening image is formed. Here, instead of burglars, the stereotype is of slovenly, morbidly obese videogamers who lie around all day drinking Mountain Dew, completely without ambition aside from securing their weed supply, all social bonds long since abandoned in favour of the next puff.

The reality is that it's not so much a matter of cannabis being addictive, as that people who do not have adequate levels of stimulation search for anything they can to fill the gap, and cannabis fills the gap. Anyone who smokes cannabis every day can tell you this – it's frequently a matter of having nothing better to do.

As was demonstrated by the Rat Park experiments carried out by Professor Bruce Alexander (6), addiction is a function of both available addictive substances and a lack of environmental stimulation.

The Rat Park experiments showed that rats that lived in a stimulating and interesting environment, where a variety of exercise, food and mating opportunities were available, were up to 19 times less likely to consume water laced with morphine when compared to rats that lived in a standard laboratory cage. Given that rats are also social (or at least semi-social) mammals, this can teach us some things about the nature of addiction in humans.

The fact is that human society of 2019 has left some people behind to die, and for these unfortunate masses there is not a lot of pleasant stimulation to be had. Some of these people turn to alcohol to fill the gap, some turn to opiates, some turn to tobacco, some turn to cannabis. In all cases, the problem is not the drug itself, but an environment that fails to provide stimulation enough to meet people's psychological needs.

If sufficiently fulfilling stimulation is available (or at least entertaining stimulation), people don't tend to smoke cannabis all day. Therefore, the emphasis shouldn't be on putting people in cages for using cannabis, it should be on creating a society that people freely want to engage in.

Most of the reason why cannabis users have had to take all the blame, instead of the people responsible for constructing society in a way that others want to escape it by using cannabis, is that the people responsible for designing society have all the power. Naturally, therefore, they design society in such a way that all of the other members of it have to take the blame for its failures.

What cannabis addiction ultimately amounts to is blaming cannabis for the problems caused by cannabis prohibition. Just because bored people with nothing to do sometimes smoke cannabis all day doesn't mean that the cannabis forced them to do it. A healthy society, one that allowed people to freely use cannabis in (e.g.) coffeeshops, would find that people soon get bored of it and drift onto other things.

The argument that cannabis is addictive is not sufficient to justify making cannabis illegal. The addictive potential of cannabis is minor, and the withdrawal symptoms from it mild. Focus should be placed on organising society in a manner that inspires ordinary people to engage with it of their own free will, not punishing cannabis use.

# 40

# Cannabis Does Not Cause Schizophrenia

One of the most common pieces of folk wisdom regarding cannabis is that it causes schizophrenia. For some reason, the one thing that every muggle seems to know about cannabis is that, if you smoke too much of it, you go crazy. Like almost everything else that muggles think they know about cannabis, this factoid is bollocks, as this examination will show.

The reason why it is commonly believed that cannabis causes schizophrenia is because of the large number of schizophrenics who smoke cannabis. It is believed that up to 25% of schizophrenics have a "cannabis use disorder", and there is certainly a strong association between the two, but it isn't because cannabis causes psychosis.

Many schizophrenics could have told you many years ago (as we did in the *Cannabis Activist's Handbook* (1)) that cannabis is medicinal for people with mental illnesses. There is currently much interest in the use of CBD (cannabidiol) medicine in the treatment of psychosis (2). Multiple scientific papers support this (3). A *Schizophrenia Bulletin* article (4) stated that "Interest in the therapeutic potential of CBD stemmed from evidence that it has broadly opposite effects to that of THC."

The most recent evidence suggests that cannabidiol has the opposite effect to THC in many ways (5). CBD appears to reduce positive symptoms (e.g. hallucinations) in schizophrenics (6), which again testifies to its medicinal qualities. It doesn't cause them – indeed, "even high doses of oral CBD do not cause psychological, psychomotor, cognitive, or physical effects that are characteristic for THC."

This recent research suggests that some of the cannabinoids in the cannabis plant, particularly CBD, have a calming and soothing effect. This effect is not necessarily limited to people with mental illnesses, but for people with mental illnesses this calming and soothing effect is certainly medicinal. Once the medicinal benefits of CBD are understood, it becomes obvious that much of the reason for the association between psychosis and cannabis is because psychotics find that ingesting the CBD in cannabis alleviates some of the suffering that comes with psychosis.

One study found that it was much more likely that predictors of schizophrenia led to cannabis use than that cannabis use led to schizophrenia (7); in other words, underlying factors that tended to cause schizophrenia also tended to cause cannabis use. Of some interest is that schizophrenia itself is a predictor of future cannabis use (8), which supports the idea that the nature of the suffering caused by the condition happens to be alleviated by cannabis. Indeed, cannabis use itself is a heritable trait.

Supporting this was a study (9) that found that "cannabis use was genetically correlated with a wide range of behaviors and personality traits, such as alcohol use and dependence, increased risk taking, and decreased conscientiousness, as well as a variety of mental health disorders."

So there is mounting evidence that underlying psychological factors explain much of the cannabis-psychosis connection. It's known that genes heavily influence many personality traits, such as openness and degree of neophilia/neophobia, and it's possible that possession of some particular traits lead naturally to both schizophrenia and to cannabis use. Personality characteristics that correlate with developing schizophrenia also correlate with future cannabis use.

Yet another study found that executive function in schizophrenics was superior if they were cannabis users (10). Examples of executive function are problem solving, working memory and cognitive flexibility. This ties in with the argument, made at length elsewhere (11), that the use of cannabis keeps the mind young and plastic. This may be especially true in the case of schizophrenics because of possible neurodegenerative effects of schizophrenia.

Many schizophrenics are able to tell you that cannabis use grants the ability to set aside certain recurring thought patterns, particularly those of the brooding or obsessive variety. It is often possible to get stuck in thought loops and ruminate if one does not have a substance that facilitates novel and original thought patterns. Something about the nature of schizophrenia makes brooding and obsessive thoughts more likely, and so it's apparent that a substance with the effects mentioned in the studies above will be of benefit to schizophrenics, and that this will cause them to use it more.

So the reality is that cannabis does not cause schizophrenia, but that factors associated with schizophrenia are also associated with cannabis use, and these underlying reasons are why schizophrenics use so much cannabis. In particular, a certain kind of mind has qualities that makes it prone to both developing a cannabis habit and developing schizophrenia. We can guess at what some of these qualities are: no doubt openness and creativity are at the forefront, as is an early childhood marked by abuse and neglect.

Most crucially, it's now more apparent than ever that cannabidiol is highly medicinal for people with schizophrenia. This is the main reason for the association between schizophrenia and cannabis use – using cannabis brings relief from the suffering that comes with conditions like schizophrenia. People with schizophrenia have long known this, which is why they continue to use it at high rates despite intense discouragement from doctors and politicians.

Not only is the argument that cannabis causes schizophrenia false, but the opposite is true. Elements of the cannabis plant act as anti-psychotics that alleviate the symptoms of psychotic disorders. Cannabis should be made legal so that those who benefit from the anxiolytic and antipsychotic properties of, e.g., cannabidiol, can get access to it for the sake of alleviating the suffering associated with their condition. This is especially true for schizophrenics, who seem to benefit greatly from CBD medicine.

# 41

# Reform Would Not Send
# The Wrong Message
# To The Children

One of the usual reasons trotted out for opposing cannabis law reform is that it "wouldn't send the right message to the kids". This was the statement that former New Zealand Prime Minister John Key frequently made to the media when pressed on the subject. As this chapter will examine, however, this thought-terminating cliche reflects a mistaken attitude.

It might sound laughable, but there are many in the New Zealand Government who believe that their personal conduct sets an example for the rest of the country to follow. These deluded fools genuinely believe that the young people of the nation look to them as an example of integrity, honesty and correct conduct. So detached from the people are they, that they are entirely unaware of the contempt in which they are held.

Some of these egomaniacs are afraid that making any move on cannabis law reform would "send the wrong message to the kids". By this, they think that liberalising the cannabis laws will lead to a spate of young people taking up cannabis use as a habit, on account of that their elders had sent them the message that it was okay.

Leaving aside the obvious retort that this would actually be a good thing if it stopped those young people from doing as much alcohol or synthetic drugs, there are a number of reasons to think that this reasoning is illogical.

For one thing, the message that our politicians appear to be sending by the example of their conduct is one of alcohol, tobacco and sleaze. If they are the ones setting the standards for the young to follow, then we can look forward to many decades of boozing, bribery, infidelity, dishonesty, backstabbing and all manner of petty quibbling and bitching to come.

For another thing, we have to ask ourselves if prohibition itself is actually a good message to be sending out.

The message that the Government seems to be sending by enforcing cannabis prohibition is that the best way to deal with drug problems is by putting people in cages. If someone has a drug dependency of some kind, the way to help them is not by giving them medical care, but by physically forcing them into a cage full of rapists, murderers and thieves.

They seem to be telling people that empathy and compassion don't factor into government decisions, and that they are more than happy to brutally force citizens to conform to arbitrary laws, even when those same citizens don't consent to them. Your body is the property of the Government, and they can do what they want with it, including put it in a cage if you use a medicine they don't approve of.

Worse, they're also sending the message that science, logic and reason don't factor into government decisions. The Government is happy to go along with foreign mass hysteria about reefer madness, and thinks it acceptable to force laws onto New Zealanders on the grounds that they have been introduced overseas, with no consideration given to the science or to the need for evidence.

Perhaps the worst message of all has been that sent by Parliamentarians who have ignored all the letters and emails they have received from their constituents about cannabis law reform. For decades, Kiwis have been entreating their Parliamentarians to do something about cannabis prohibition, knowing how much access to cannabis medicine would improve their life quality. And for decades, those Parliamentarians did nothing – the vast majority too cowardly to even raise a peep.

By ignoring the will of the people for cannabis reform, the Government is sending the message that it's acceptable for them to impose whatever arbitrary laws it likes on the population, even without that population's consent, and then to ignore them when they complain about the suffering caused. This is far more of a danger than the risk of Parliamentarians sending the message that it's okay to use cannabis.

If the Government is truly concerned about the message that their conduct sends to the people, they ought to legalise cannabis today, and make an apology for all the suffering their actions caused by waging a War on Drugs against their own people. This would send a message of humility, integrity and contrition – much better than imprisoning people for using a substance that the New Zealand people think should be legal.

# 42

# Cannabis Does Not Make People Impotent

Everyone by now has seen the propaganda image on the back of the tobacco packet that depicts a droopy cigarette, imitating erectile dysfunction. Cannabis has undergone a similar propaganda attack, with many people coming to believe that cannabis can make people impotent. This chapter shows that the truth, once again, is very different to what we have been told.

Like many things that the authorities want to forbid, cannabis has variously been blamed for pretty much everything that could go wrong in a person's life. Cannabis causes psychosis, it causes cancer, it causes crime, and we're also told that it makes people impotent.

Now, it's certainly true that smoking things is not healthy. Smoking anything, cannabis or tobacco, leads to unhealthy lungs and worse circulation. It also leads to heart disease. All of this makes it much harder for smokers to get healthy erections, as this is a function of the health of the circulatory system.

It's also true that not all cannabis users are healthy. Part of the reason for this is because they smoke things (as mentioned above), but most of the reason is that cannabis is a medicine, and medicines are not typically used by healthy people. People who aren't healthy also tend to be sexually dysfunctional, for obvious reasons, so there's a clear reason to expect the presence of a link between the two.

However, the simple truth is that cannabis, by itself, does not make people impotent. In fact, like so many of the things that people have come to believe about cannabis on account of the propaganda, the truth is closer to the opposite of what we have been told. Cannabis is actually an aphrodisiac, and has been employed as such for a very long time.

Indeed, cannabis has been known to be an aphrodisiac for millennia. There are references to it in Ayurvedic folk medicine from 2,500 years ago (1), and its use as an aphrodisiac may be as much as 3,000 years old (2). The efficacy of cannabis for such purposes is well-known among young and free-thinking people today.

There are several reasons for this, as any hippie could tell you. Most of the reasons are psychological, the most obvious being one that cannabis shares with alcohol: it's an anxiolytic. People are often too physically anxious and wound up to be able to make love, because their bodies are in fight mode, and so being touched releases cortisol instead of oxytocin.

Cannabis can change that by putting a person into a calmer, more relaxed mood. It can have the effect of stopping runaway, neurotic or aggressive thoughts and replacing them with more placid and appreciative feelings. Cannabis has the ability to get people into the right mood for sex, probably a combination of its anxiolytic effects and the increased physical sensitivity it offers.

Another psychological obstacle to enjoying the sexual experience is deep religious brainwashing in childhood. Many people have been deeply conditioned, since early childhood, to believe that sex was evil and that enjoying the sexual impulse was an act of evil. For some of these people, it's no longer possible to enjoy having sex while in a normal state of mind.

Yet another common psychological obstacle is previous sexual trauma. Many women who have been sexually molested or raped have difficulty letting go of the trauma enough to trust a man in bed. Likewise, many men find it difficult to achieve the desired level of responsiveness on account of previous humiliations. These kinds of prior traumas often make it difficult for a person to properly enjoy having sex.

Cannabis can help overcome all of these obstacles, thanks to the deconditioning effect that it has on the mind. Because cannabis is good for breaking down old thought patterns, it can break down the conditioned emotional response that occurs when a person is exposed to a stimulus that reminds them of a previous trauma.

One reason why cannabis has become associated with psychosis is because it makes people more open and more willing to explore. This is also one of the reasons why cannabis does the opposite of making people impotent. Sometimes a person is closed off to the idea of intimacy, and not because of trauma or any of the above reasons, but from sheer natural boringness. Cannabis can be what's needed to open such a person up.

Of course, all this is part of the reason why cannabis was banned in the first place. It's the basis for the "Reefer makes darkies think they're as good as white men" comment that led to the prohibition of cannabis (3). The deconditioning effect of cannabis is a danger to those who benefit from the initial conditioning. Those brainwashers have a profound influence on our lawmakers.

Again, the correct approach must be one that maximises freedom while minimising new danger and risk. The apparent paradox that daily cannabis use can decrease sexual function, while occasional cannabis use can increase it, needs to be recognised. This can only become possible if our current dishonest approach to cannabis is replaced with an honest one.

From there, it will be possible to both get medical treatment for those who use too much cannabis, and to get medical treatment for those who have problems with impotency and who could benefit from cannabis. The humane thing to do would be to legalise it so that people can get the help they need, when they need it, without interference from the law.

# 43

# Amotivational Syndrome Is Not Reason To Prohibit Cannabis

One of the major harms of cannabis, we are told, is the dreaded amotivational syndrome. This raises the spectre of A students and gifted athletes who get the reefer madness and end up lying around on the couch all day watching television and playing with themselves. As with many arguments for cannabis prohibition, this one is based upon a sliver of truth, blown out of proportion.

According to a 1983 paper in the *Journal of Psychoactive Drugs* (1), the supposedly characteristic symptoms of amotivational syndrome are general passivity and apathy, loss of desire to work or to be productive, loss of energy, depression, moodiness, lack of stress tolerance and slovenliness.

If you think that this sounds like most mental illnesses, and that a person with these problems probably uses cannabis as a medicine to deal with a mental illness, you'd be right – for the most part.

However, there is such a thing as amotivational syndrome.

It's worth noting here that this book is not about advocating for cannabis use per se. This book advocates for a reduction in human suffering by way of repealing cannabis prohibition. So there's no problem in admitting that it's entirely possible that cannabis smoking is a bad idea for a particular individual, and that there are many situations where many people shouldn't use it.

The neurobiology of amotivational syndrome is not difficult to understand, because it's essentially the same thing as burnout.

Amotivational syndrome can arise when a person gets so high, for so long, that their brain circuitry gets used to that greater level of stimulation. This can lead to a situation where a person is no longer receptive to normal sources of stimulation.

Most people can relate to this feeling. After all, it's little different to the same burnout a person gets after partying too long or being too long in combat or under high levels of stress. Studies have shown decreased response sensitivity after periods of heavy cannabis use, but this is only part of the story.

As is the case with tobacco, decreased response sensitivity is often the reason why people use cannabis. For many people, the decreased sensitivity that comes with cannabis use is what they feel is keeping them sane. These people use cannabis so that they are more relaxed and calm when they have to interact with others.

Thus, amotivational syndrome is far from a good reason to make cannabis illegal. In fact, it's even more support in favour of legalisation.

Because some strains decrease sensitivity, while other strains appear to increase it, the best approach is to let people safely experiment with accurately and clearly labelled products purchased from a legal supplier, so that they can find the right proportion of cannabinoids for them. If amotivational syndrome is a problem, it can be best be avoided by avoiding those high-THC, low-CBD strains that tend to overload the mind.

Another point worth emphasising here is that one culture's "amotivational syndrome" is another culture's correct level of relaxation.

This was written about as far back as 1976, when a study pointed out that Jamaican culture had no concept of amotivational syndrome (2). That study refutes the idea of amotivational syndrome more generally, pointing out that the very idea of it is rooted in prejudice against cannabis users (as is the idea that cannabis causes psychosis).

It's already clear that the rate at which our societies are consuming the natural resources of the Earth is not sustainable. The 8 billion people on this planet cannot sustainably consume more resources than does the average Western beneficiary (3), and these limits are not the result of political forces but hard natural ones. These inexorable forces pose immense problems for our culture in the West, which glorifies production and consumption.

It could be that, far from being destroyed by laziness and apathy, cannabis users have simply reduced their consumption to sustainable levels. The motivation to do this perhaps arose through a greater appreciation of the interdependence of all life on Earth, a common consequence of cannabis use.

Amotivational syndrome, then, could be said to only be a problem in the context of a modern society that demands maximum productivity from everyone. So the unwillingness to work and to be productive might really be a turn away from the consumption mania of the industrialised world and a return to the sanity that existed before it (when many people used cannabis regularly).

In any case, the best way to deal with all this is to tell people the truth. If it's true that high-THC strains of cannabis overload the brain's reward pathways and make them insensitive to everyday stimuli, then this needs to be explained honestly to people. Conversely, if a person is happy using cannabis so that they become more relaxed and don't consume the planet as voraciously, that also needs to be accepted.

If the Government and its departments told the truth about cannabis, then people would have confidence that their doctors were telling the truth when they tried to explain amotivational syndrome. This would make it far more likely that those who had proper cause to stop using cannabis would listen to people advising them to do so.

# 44

# Cannabis Does Not Lead To Crime

One of the reasons offered by prohibitionists for keeping cannabis illegal is that cannabis leads to crime, by way of some quality inherent to itself. This is a favourite reason trotted out by people whose livelihoods are dependent on government funding for cannabis prohibition, people who are often pigs at the trough in more than one sense (1). The truth is not only that cannabis is not criminogenic by itself, but that cannabis prohibition is what has caused criminal behaviour to become related to the substance.

One common line of horseshit that people often hear with regard to cannabis use is that it warps people's brains and makes them impulsive, and thereby criminal. By means of some nebulous kind of brain damage, people who use cannabis lose their ability to control their own inner malice and naturally come to start abusing themselves and other people, both mentally and physically. They come to commit crimes of opportunity when they would normally have resisted the impulse to do so.

Another stupidity is that cannabis addiction leads to stealing to service the cost of the addiction. Confusing cannabis users with the worst kind of crack or heroin user, this stereotype has it that legal cannabis would lead to a large number of people becoming addicted to it and then stealing from other people to get the money to buy more cannabis. Ignoring the fact that finding a dealer who has a proper supply is many times harder than getting enough money to buy the weed in the first place, this idea suggests that prohibition is good because it leads to fewer burglaries and muggings.

The fact is that neither of these glib just-so stories is true.

There is indeed, a link between cannabis and crime, and it comes from the criminal associations that have to be made in order to maintain a cannabis supply. Because cannabis is illegal, the only people that can supply it regularly are professional criminals. So a person who has a need for medicinal cannabis has to deal with professional criminals on account of that they are forbidden by law to deal with a pharmacist.

It is true that, when a person who needs a regular supply of medicinal cannabis comes into contact with a professional criminal, this can lead to crime. What is also true is that this criminogenic effect is a consequence of cannabis prohibition, and has nothing to do with the nature of cannabis itself. The professional criminal might expose the cannabis user to other drugs, or to illegal firearms, or to stolen goods, or even to blackmail. This is a result of the fact that only criminals deal in cannabis when it's illegal.

Cannabis doesn't make people stab and rob other people by itself. Going without cannabis, much like going without other psychiatric medicines, mostly just puts people in shitty moods and carries a risk of psychosis. But if you're the sort of person that does stab and rob people, then its almost a certainty that either you are involved with cannabis or that you move in the same circles as someone who does.

So it's true that there is an association between cannabis and crime. But this association can be explained by the fact that both are illegal, rather than that involvement with cannabis inherently causes criminal conduct. In places where cannabis is legal, as it (sort of) has been in the Netherlands for some decades now, people who want small amounts of cannabis – even if they want it regularly – can get it without coming into contact with the criminal underworld.

As a result, cannabis does not lead to exposure to harmful criminal activity in places where it is legal at the same rate as it does in places where it is illegal.

Because of all this, we can state that the truth is really close to the opposite of what's commonly said. A *Forbes* article from earlier this year (2) showed that crime had fallen in Mexican states that border America, on account of that cannabis law reform had taken the cannabis trade away from the black market. Homicides related to the drug trade were believed to have fallen 41% because of cannabis law reform, as incidents of turf wars over illegal cannabis sales essentially vanished.

These statistics reveal a couple of things. Not only does cannabis not inherently lead to crime, but cannabis prohibition itself inherently leads to crime. Prohibiting cannabis is to move it onto the black market, which is to ensure that organised crime will fight over territory and distribution profits. Once there are large, black market profits to be made in the trade of an illicit substance, ensuing violence is all but guaranteed.

The laws against cannabis prohibition can only be supported if a person understands nothing of the crime wave that followed in the wake of alcohol prohibition. Cannabis prohibition takes all the legitimate demand for the substance – and the demand for it is legitimate, not "drug addiction" – then gifts all of that demand to the black market, who are the only people willing to supply it. This means that it's prohibition that causes the crime that is associated with cannabis, and not the cannabis itself.

Cannabis law reform is necessary so that people who want to engage in the cannabis trade are not exposed to the criminal underworld. This will reduce crime rates by keeping citizens who would otherwise be law-abiding away from the sort of professional criminal who might take advantage of them, or who might bring their criminal influence into other areas of the cannabis user's life.

# 45

# It Doesn't Matter That High-THC Strains Now Exist

A prohibitionist argument beloved of the Police is that cannabis should stay illegal because it now contains much more THC than it used to. This is commonly employed as a counterargument to imply that, even though the dangers of cannabis use have been massively exaggerated, it should still be illegal, because the warnings have become accurate over time.

One particular BBC article provides a good example of the ridiculous propaganda that people have been exposed to over the years (1). It claims that "high-potency cannabis or skunk" is a completely different form of cannabis to the herbal cannabis that people usually smoke. This is done in an effort to make people think that the threat posed by legalisation is categorically more extreme than it was in the past.

It's true that some cannabis strains today are much, much stronger than what used to exist, despite the nostalgic recollections of old hippies. Breeders have had decades to experiment with these strains, and some of them have cultivated varieties that are much higher in THC than anything that could have existed previously.

Because a high-THC strain will offer more of a buzz per unit of volume, it naturally makes for a superior product from a criminal point of view. The greater the buzz per unit of volume, the easier it is to transport, to hide and to smuggle. Black market dealers can charge more if their product gets a reputation for being superpowered, and all of this has caused high-THC strains to dominate the market in many places.

Although it's true that a high-THC strain of cannabis can create unwanted reactions, particularly by producing a more intense experience than desired, this is only a problem if cannabis is sold on the black market. Like many of the arguments for cannabis prohibition that appeal to the harms of cannabis, further investigation shows that the harm is caused by prohibition and not by cannabis itself.

A high-THC strain of cannabis can get a person stoned faster than a low-THC strain, and perhaps also more heavily, but this is not anything close to a legitimate argument in favour of cannabis prohibition. The safest way to protect people from getting a more intense buzz than they wanted is actually to legalise cannabis, for two reasons.

Legal, properly regulated cannabis means that whatever a person consumes must be clearly labelled with a cannabinoid profile. This means that the user will know what they're getting. If a person is inexperienced with cannabis they might want specifically to avoid a high-THC strain or to use a high-CBD strain. Even if they are experienced, they might want to know they're using a high-CBD strain.

As mentioned elsewhere, only legal cannabis can make this possible, because only cannabis produced by legitimate white market professionals will be tested and analysed to determine its precise cannabinoid profile. Therefore, only legal cannabis can ensure that the user knows what they're getting and can take the appropriate measures.

This approach synergises with having honest education about cannabis use at high school level. In the same way the high schoolers are educated about sex, driving and alcohol, an honest approach would see them educated about cannabis as well. Part of this approach would involve being told that high-THC strains can provoke effects that are more powerful than intended.

The second reason is that regulating cannabis makes it possible to pass a law, as has been done in some American jurisdictions, so that the recreational cannabis being sold in shops must contain a minimum percentage of CBD. This is done with the intent of minimising psychotic responses, as there is evidence that the CBD in cannabis has an anti-psychotic effect that balances the psychotogenic effect of the THC (2).

Regulation means that the circumstances in which people use cannabis can be controlled with a view to preventing adverse outcomes such as overdoses on super high-THC skunk. Even if it was not deemed necessary to legislate for a minimum CBD level for all cannabis, it could be ensured that the cannabis consumed publicly in cafes had such a limitation.

Prohibiting cannabis because of the fear of high-THC strains is like prohibiting alcohol because absinthe exists. It's a dumb move that just leads to more suffering in the end. It would be much better to legalise cannabis so that people both knew how to use cannabis properly and also the chemical makeup of any strain they may wish to use.

# 46

# It Doesn't Matter That People Have To Pay For Cannabis Users' Healthcare

One argument that is often made by people in response to proposals for cannabis law reform is that they don't want to pay for cannabis users' healthcare. The logic goes that cannabis law reform is unfair on the general populace, because they have to fork out for the inevitable increased healthcare burden through general taxation. Like the other arguments against cannabis law reform, this is mistaken.

As with so many of the false arguments against cannabis law reform, this one relies on another bogeyman. In this case, it's the supposedly heavy burden that the health system would suffer under if cannabis were to be made legal. This burden would have to be borne by everyone, and it isn't fair to expect them to do so.

As with many examples of false logic, this argument depends on seeing the situation incorrectly.

For one thing, it's possible that, if cannabis were to become legal, some of the adverse consequences of its use would become more widespread. But it's foolish to think that, in such a case, cannabis use would go up while the rates of all other recreational drugs would stay the same.

In reality, recreational cannabis is a competing good to alcohol. A lot of people use it because they find the ritual of rolling up and smoking a joint as relaxing and enjoyable as drinking a beer, and at least as social. Everywhere that cannabis is legal, at least some of the population have decided that they prefer to socialise over some weed than over some booze.

So the supposed "extra" healthcare burden that would be caused by increased cannabis use is balanced, perhaps even several times over, by the savings that accrue from health problems that were prevented by the reduced use of other recreational drugs.

Alcohol abuse is believed to cost New Zealand $4.9 billion per year (1). The total cost of cannabis use on the New Zealand healthcare system right now is, even if one uses the ultra-conservative Drug Harm Index (2), $431 million (3). This latter figure is not merely the cost of cannabis use to the healthcare system but also ancillary costs, so the true figure is much lower (this latter figure also includes $126 million of costs due to premature death caused by cannabis use and is therefore somewhat fantastical).

So even if legal cannabis doubled the total harm that the Drug Harm Index says that cannabis does to society, this would be more than compensated for if it reduced the total harm done by alcohol by 10% or more.

A second factor to consider is that the cost of cannabis damage is small compared to the cost of old people just clinging onto life for a few more years.

New Zealand's total healthcare expenditure was $16.8 billion last year (4), and people aged over 65 used over 42% of that (5) – and that percentage is increasing. So people over 65 use roughly $8 billion dollars worth of taxpayers' money on health costs every year, much of which is wasted on futile attempts to delay a terminal illness.

Even if we ignore that cannabis use is not higher in jurisdictions where it is legal, and even if we ignore that legal cannabis would mean users could use much less harmful routes of administration, and even if we assume that the total healthcare damage would be double under legalisation than what it is now, it still wouldn't be a great amount of money compared to what is already spent.

The third argument is, of course, that it simply doesn't matter if cannabis users' healthcare has to be paid for out of general taxation. As mentioned above, alcohol abuse costs New Zealand almost five billion dollars a year, which amounts to close to $1,600 per taxpayer. If such a high bar is acceptable for alcohol, then its acceptable for cannabis as well.

Cannabis users are, or should be, part of our society the same way as anyone else is. So in the same way that we're happy to pay for the healthcare costs of cigarette smokers, alcohol drinkers, Olanzapine takers (the side-effects of many psychiatric medicines are bad for physical health), rugby players, horse riders and mountain climbers, so too should we be happy to pay for the healthcare costs of cannabis users.

Legal cannabis would make it easier to minimise healthcare costs anyway, because doctors would be able to encourage cannabis users to avoid joints and dabs in favour of edibles and vapourisers. So if healthcare costs really are a concern, legal cannabis is better for more than one reason.

In summary, it's not fair to object to cannabis law reform on the basis that the general taxpayer would have to pay for a sudden massive healthcare burden. A repeal of cannabis prohibition would not lead to such a burden – in fact, a sober look at the experience suggests the overall healthcare cost of recreational drug use would fall if cannabis became legal.

# 47

# Legalisation Is Better For The Environment

Recent studies suggest that the future prospects for Earth's environment are poor. The situation is dire enough that, finally, an awareness is growing that certain measures will have to be taken (1) if the human species is to survive – and soon. Cannabis law reform is one of those measures (if a minor one).

Many people labour under the idea that cannabis prohibition stops people from using cannabis. Therefore, they assume, cannabis prohibition prevents it from being grown and used. The truth, of course, is that evil laws don't prevent actions, because human nature is to defy evil laws, and so people grow cannabis everywhere anyway. In any case, cannabis is a medicine, and people will not simply go without a medicine because of the law.

Because of things like Police helicopters that go searching the hills and forests for outdoor grows, a majority of people who grow cannabis do so indoors, and most of these grows are simple setups under a 400 or 600 Watt bulb. These generally cost somewhere between $70 and $100 a month to run, and can produce several ounces of weed over a eight- or ten-week cycle.

This is a great outcome for an individual cannabis user who doesn't want to deal with the black market, but it's not the best outcome for the environment.

A study by American scientist Evan Mills found that indoor cannabis grows use up to 1% of America's entire energy supply (2). If a similar proportion holds true in New Zealand, it would mean that indoor cannabis grows in New Zealand suck up electricity equivalent to that used by a city the size of Nelson every year. This represents some $60 million worth of electricity, every year.

Another way to put this: a four-plant grow uses as much electricity as running 29 refrigerators. It's a lot of energy being used for something that doesn't really need to happen. After all, these grows are only done indoors for the sake of evading detection.

Legal cannabis would mean that cannabis growers could simply put a plant outside and let it grow in the Sun, without fear of being spotted by Police helicopters. There would be no energy requirements at all, and the cost of grow nutrients and the like would be minimal on account of that the plant would just be allowed to grow as large as possible.

Not all indoor cannabis growing could immediately be switched to outdoors. Many people simply don't have the appropriate facilities. However, the vast majority of it could be, on account of that people would rather buy cannabis from a shop or get it from a pharmacy than grow it themselves, for a greater cost, and have to worry about watering, spider mites, replacement bulbs, buying potting mix, getting ripped off etc.

So legal cannabis would mean that companies would be able to build entire outdoor cannabis farms, and these farms would be much better for the environment than the current arrangement, in which everyone has a home grow operation because they can't buy it legally and they need to avoid getting arrested. All of those highly inefficient home grows can be wound down in favour of commercial operations that achieve economies of scale.

The tricky thing about this argument is that the sort of person who cares about the environment already knows that cannabis should be legal. In much the same way that anyone who has bothered to look at the climate science knows that changes need to be made, anyone who has bothered to look at the science behind cannabis knew that cannabis prohibition should have been repealed 20 years ago.

The sort of people who genuinely believe that it's a good idea to put people in cages for growing or using cannabis are, almost inevitably, the same kind of people who don't care at all about the environment or what the state of it might be after we are gone. The characteristic feature of such people is an absence of empathy for others, and an inability to consider their suffering to be real. So the environmental argument will convince few who are not already convinced.

However, the fact remains that cannabis law reform is a better move for the environment. It would greatly reduce the carbon footprint of the cannabis cultivation industry, as well as reducing the amount of wastage elsewhere. Given the pressing need to consider environmental impacts in all areas, we should make it legal for individuals to grow cannabis outside at home.

# 48

# A Majority Now Want Reform

One of the strongest arguments for cannabis prohibition was that it was what the majority wanted. For better or for worse, we live in a democratic system, which means that the law ought to reflect the collective wisdom of the majority, and opinion polling in Western countries used to favour cannabis prohibition. This is, however, no longer the case.

It's true that opinion polls used to favour prohibition. In 1969 only 13% of Americans believed that cannabis should be legal. Only 44% of Americans believed that cannabis should be legal as recently as 2009. By 2018, however, opinion polls now favour legalisation (1). 66% of Americans now support legal recreational cannabis along the lines of the Colorado model, and the trend line points sharply upwards.

If one goes back 100 years, most people thought that cannabis should be legal anyway, as its medicinal applications were obvious. Cannabis prohibition is the experimental condition, and it has failed. So this sharp decrease in prohibitionist sentiment over recent years is really a return to the baseline condition of liberal cannabis sentiment.

The public did consent to the experiment with prohibition, this is true, but this was the result of a naive people believing the lies of politicians beholden to industries that saw cannabis as a competitor to be suppressed. Foremost among these were the timber, alcohol and pharmaceutical industries. Being the paid whores that they are, Western politicians happily told lies about how cannabis had no medicinal value and was a dangerous drug, because their sponsors profitted from it.

As a result of these decades of lies, the public has not been accurately informed. As a result of that, they could not make correct decisions. Because politicians have been lying to people for decades about cannabis, there has arisen a common perception about cannabis that has been difficult to correct. When the public are accurately informed, things are different.

If people are correctly informed about cannabis, with reference to science, evidence and reality, they almost always come down on the side of legalisation. There is simply no scientific evidence supporting any of the common arguments about cannabis causing violent murders, rapes and general madness. The mid-1990s repeal movement in California associated with Proposition 215 (2) was possibly the first time that a proper public attempt to tell the truth about cannabis had ever been made, and in that instance they came down on the side of legalisation.

As mentioned above, a clear majority of Americans are now in favour of legal cannabis, and something similar can be observed in Britain (3), as well as New Zealand. Although opinion polling about New Zealand's upcoming cannabis referendum is rudimentary on account of that the actual referendum question is yet to be formulated, what little there is suggests that the pro-cannabis side is already ahead (4). Probably it will pull further ahead as more positive news comes in from American states that have legalised.

Other opinion polls, asking more specific questions, have returned similar results in New Zealand. A Drug Foundation survey conducted in July (5) found that two-thirds of the country wanted some kind of change to the cannabis laws, although they were not given a clear distinction between legalisation and decriminalisation. It also found that the prohibitionist side was no longer winning the recreational cannabis debate.

The next generation of young people is heavily pro cannabis all over the West, as described in *Understanding New Zealand* (6). McGlashan calculated that the correlation between being under 20 and voting for the Aotearoa Legalise Cannabis Party was 0.41, whereas the correlation between being aged 65+ and voting for that party was -0.43. This means that the opponents to cannabis law reform are all dying off: after all, society advances one funeral at a time.

What this suggests is that the victory of cannabis law reform is inevitable. The fact is that the majority of anti-cannabis sentiment is held by brainwashed old people who will not long be with us. There is already a general majority in favour of cannabis law reform, and this will only grow stronger as time progresses and old people who have been conditioned to hate cannabis users die.

Cannabis ought to be legal because a majority of people have now realised that the fears were grossly overblown and they want reform. Cannabis prohibition no longer has the support of the people, and support for it continues to fall. In a short number of years there will only be a remnant of cannabis prohibitionists left, and it might be better to put them out of their misery now.

# 49

## One Person Who Smoked Cannabis And Went Crazy Is Not A Pattern

If one talks to many prohibitionists, an argument that comes up over and over again is the argument from personal experience. They will tell a story about how they knew a person who was doing great, until one day they smoked cannabis and just went crazy. This chapter explains why this is not a legitimate reason to keep cannabis illegal.

It's a familiar story by now. The sedulous medical student, the hard-working businessman or the devoted mother, all living amazing lives until they had a smoke of cannabis and then – boom, total mental collapse. It's a story familiar to anyone who has seen the film *Trainspotting*, only it doesn't really happen that way with cannabis.

It's true that the use of cannabis often occurs at the same time that a person becomes a psychiatric casualty. Inevitably, however, further examination of the lives of these people show that things aren't as simple as use cannabis, go crazy.

Psychosis isn't normally something that just breaks out from nowhere. Usually it's something that develops, quickly or slowly, over a period of time, during which the person becomes more and more agitated. In most cases when psychosis is preceded by cannabis use, there are multiple factors at play, in particular lack of sleep, anxiety, adrenaline and job, health or relationship stresses.

When a person hears about someone they know using cannabis and then having a psychiatric event, what they don't also hear about is the surrounding life circumstances. Almost always, the supposedly "healthy" person was either starting to feel overwhelmed with the pressure and stress in their lives (which is what turned them to cannabis) or there was a pre-existing psychiatric condition that wasn't known about and which was exacerbated by cannabis use.

More academically, it is said that the plural of anecdote is not data. Knowing that one person who had a psychotic break happened to have used cannabis at some point leading up to it is one thing. It is not, however, evidence that a wider pattern exists of perfectly healthy people using cannabis and then becoming psychotic.

Even more academically, arguing that cannabis should be illegal because you knew one person who smoked it and went crazy is an example of the fallacy of composition. This is a logical fallacy that states that something that is true of one member of a group (such as one cannabis user) is true of the entire group (all cannabis users).

In other words, even if was true that there was one person who did become psychotic purely on account of cannabis use and no other factor, it wouldn't make it possible to generalise this experience onto all people who use cannabis. One example is just one example, and it requires many further such examples before one can conclude that using cannabis inevitably leads to psychosis.

However, it's entirely possible that using cannabis can contribute to psychosis under certain circumstances.

The first common way is that it can bring up traumatic memories. A large number of people, perhaps even a majority, have some kind of suppressed memory. Usually this relates to an early childhood trauma, with violence and sexual assault being the most common. The percolating effect of cannabis on the thoughts can cause such repressed traumas to bubble to the surface, and often in contexts where the user is not prepared for them.

Many people have been forced to suppress these memories in order to have a chance at an ordinary life. So when they suddenly face them again, the stress of this can lead to an episode of mental disturbance. This is particularly true if the memory cannot easily be suppressed again.

The second common way is that it can bring the user into spiritual realms of thought that they may not be prepared for. As discussed at length elsewhere in Chapter 22, cannabis is a spiritual sacrament. The dangerous side of this is when people use it expecting a high, and instead find themselves confronted with deep existential or spiritual questions.

It's normal for people to avoid thinking about the fact that they're going to die one day. One of the most common ways to break this habit is to have a smoke of cannabis and find one's mind drifting to unusual places. The deconditioning effect of cannabis can have a greatly beneficial effect on creativity, but push it too far and you can lose touch with the bonds tethering you to collective reality.

Neither of these common ways can be helped by making cannabis illegal. Pushing cannabis underground has only had the effect of making people unaware of the real psychological effects of the substance, and this lack of proper awareness has caused more damage than cannabis itself.

In any case, given the large numbers of people who do use cannabis in New Zealand, and the large numbers of mentally ill people in New Zealand, it's not surprising for someone to know a person who is in both of these categories. If someone did know a person who used cannabis and later became mentally ill, that's not indicative of a wider pattern.

Furthermore, this argument ignores all the people who use cannabis and don't go crazy. If 11% of the population has used cannabis within the past 12 months (1), that's a huge number of people. It means that the average person probably knows a couple of dozen cannabis users. If this is the case, then it's notable that they only knew one person who seemed to have a psychotic episode linked with cannabis use.

# 50

# Fears Of A 'Big Cannabis' Lobby Are Overblown

One of the latest scaremongering tactics is to equate the potential future harms of cannabis with the past harms of tobacco. This tactic evokes the spectre of the Big Tobacco industry and implies that legal cannabis will cause another such monster to arise. This particular trick is a favourite of the sort of prohibitionists who appeal to wowsers, such as certain religious types.

It's impossible to deny that, with the legalisation of cannabis, there will come a number of bad things. In almost every case, however, these bad things will replace even worse things that already existed. As mentioned at various points in this book, cannabis is a substitute for other substances. This is also true at the lobbyist level.

Yes, legal cannabis would strengthen the power of the cannabis lobby. Yes, this cannabis lobby will likely be as unscrupulous as the other lobbyists: they will bribe, they will lie, they will propagandise, and they will try to open access to their product while restricting access to their competitors. This outcome is unavoidable if cannabis users are to be offered equality with users of other substances.

However, the simple fact remains that they are lobbying for a product that does much less physical, mental and social harm than either alcohol or tobacco. From a harm reduction point of view, it's not a bad thing for Big Cannabis to come onto the scene if it means commensurate losses for Big Tobacco and Big Alcohol.

In any case, cannabis can never become like tobacco, for a number of reasons.

The most obvious is that people don't smoke cannabis like tobacco. It's common for a tobacco smoker to go through a pack of 30 every day, which equates to one cigarette every half an hour or so. Not even the most dedicated stoner can rip through properly-sized joints at the rate of one every half an hour.

It's impossible to smoke cannabis like this because of the psychoactive effect. After three joints, even those with the highest degree of cannabis tolerance will be feeling satisfied. As anyone who has smoked both tobacco and cannabis will attest, smoking cannabis doesn't lead to feeling pain when breathing first thing in the morning, but tobacco does.

Another major reason is that a lot of people prefer to ingest cannabis using methods other than smoking. Because cannabis prohibition attacks the infrastructure that would otherwise supply cannabis to people, it's usually sold in unprocessed form as dried buds. Thus, prohibition is the reason why cannabis culture revolves around smoking it at present.

Legal cannabis won't necessarily mean people rocking up to the dairy first thing in the morning for a pack of 25 joints that they will chainsmoke throughout the day. It will mean that people take advantage of the panoply of alternatives to smoking that will become available. People who just want a background buzz will be able to use a small amount of an edible, and people who don't want the ritual of smoking might be happy with a vapouriser.

A third reason is that it's much easier to give up using cannabis. Many cannabis users find themselves taking tolerance breaks on occasion, or even going without for several months for a change in lifestyle or to go overseas. Very rarely does a person find themselves wishing that they could just stop smoking cannabis (the usual problem is finding enough cannabis).

This is a major distinction from tobacco. According to some studies (1), a heavy majority of tobacco smokers at any point in time wish they could give up the habit, but find that they can't seem to stop because they keep feeling compelled to smoke another cigarette. This is ideal from Big Tobacco's point of view, because they will keep buying them forever, often until they die.

So there won't be a Big Cannabis trying to get people addicted to their product to milk them for decades of future sales. There doesn't need to be – cannabis sells itself. In any case, a proper introduction of legal cannabis would mean that many people would be growing it at home.

Related to this is an argument that many make: there's no point in legalising cannabis because we're trying to prevent smoking in general. This argument almost completely misses the point, which is that the major reason why cannabis gets consumed in smoked form in the first place is that it is illegal.

Legalisation would make it easier to avoid smoking cannabis for the many who prefer not to smoke it. It would make it much easier to buy pre-prepared edibles, or vapouriser pens that use oil cartridges, or just plain vapourisers that vapourise bud (which can then be baked into an edible). So from the perspective of reducing the harm caused by using cannabis, legalisation makes more sense than further prohibition.

Correctly learning from the lessons of history would mean accepting that total prohibition fails, as shown by the example of alcohol, and total legalisation fails, as shown by the example of tobacco, so therefore some light regulation is the correct and appropriate middle ground.

Light regulation would mean that the potential damage caused by Big Cannabis lobbyists was kept to a minimum, without being so restrictive that the black market would rise up again. If intelligence was applied to drafting a cannabis law that sought to minimise suffering, it would keep the excessive aspects of both legalisation and prohibition out of the equation.

# 51

# The Criminal Justice System Is Not A Treatment Pathway

Of all the terrible arguments made in favour of cannabis prohibition – and there are many – one of the worst is the argument that contends that cannabis prohibition is a good thing because some of the people that get involved in the criminal justice system are incentivised to stop using cannabis. This argument is severely flawed for a number of reasons.

One of the saddest peasant attitudes remaining in our society is the idea that certain people just need a "good kick up the arse" to encourage them to function properly again. The idea seems to be that a "short, sharp shock" of physical abuse can be beneficial to drive dullness from a person's mind. It's an abusive attitude that is a remnant of a less enlightened time and, fortunately for the rest of us, it's dying off.

This attitude finds expression in the idea that getting arrested on account of a cannabis offence could be a good thing, if that led to a person suddenly appreciating the consequences of cannabis use and changing their habits for the better.

There is an element of logic to this line of reasoning. After all, it's common for young petty criminals to become afraid the first time they encounter some genuine heat from the Police, or the first time they do a custodial sentence and realise that prison isn't a great deal of fun after all. This fear can, indeed, change behaviour.

But what this approach leaves out is two things.

The first is that many people simply don't want to stop smoking cannabis, any more than they want to stop playing rugby or buying magazines with Harry and Meghan on the cover. You could instruct the Police to arrest people for playing rugby in the park, on the grounds that their behaviour was recklessly dangerous, but it wouldn't make it the right thing to do or a good idea. Neither would it stop people from doing it.

Psychologically speaking, it's hard to declare that you know how another adult should live their lives, and so much better than them, that you can fairly justify setting the Police on them if they don't do what you say they should do. In another time and place, that degree of coercion would be recognised as slavery, and it's no wonder that people naturally disobey the cannabis laws today.

So this means that deploying the Police to force people into getting medical treatment for using cannabis (as if that even made sense) will not be effective in the long term. People feel like they have the right to use cannabis, and they will continue to feel as if they have the right, because it's natural to think it ridiculous that a medicinal plant could be illegal.

It's possible that Police involvement in a person's life might reduce their level of cannabis use, but so what? Punching someone in the face for eating a Big Mac might also inspire them to make healthier lifestyle decisions, but that doesn't mean that the overall benefit of the action outweighs the overall harm.

The second thing is that there are cases of legitimate medicinal need, and encounters with the criminal justice system are not helpful in cases of medicinal need. Police officers are not qualified doctors and neither can they be. Having them as the first line of dealing with cannabis users makes as much sense as making the Army responsible for it.

The argument refuted in this chapter is usually made by people who are entirely unaware of the medicinal properties of cannabis. When they do become aware of the medicinal properties of cannabis, they tend to stop making it. Of course, if a substance really is medicinal then it ought to be something supplied by doctors and pharmacies; the Police should not be needed at any stage.

There may, indeed, be cases where there is a cannabis user who needs psychiatric intervention. After all, there are many instances in which certain strains of cannabis will not be helpful. A person who is acutely psychotic from sleep deprivation doesn't need a honking high-THC strain that will wire them even tighter.

But even in cases like this, it's not Police intervention that would be helpful, unless it comes as part of the Mental Health Act or similar and not as part of enforcing the law against the "crime" of cannabis. A person who has mentally disintegrated so far that they need psychiatric intervention is already in a kind of hell. The last thing they need is to encounter law enforcement.

The argument that cannabis users can be persuaded to get treatment for "cannabis abuse" by getting arrested, and then threatened with further attacks from the Justice system, is neither fair nor rational. It would be better for cannabis to be made legal and destigmatised, so that people who did need treatment would be more likely to get it. Police involvement is unnecessary.

# 52

# Legalisation Would Not Increase Drugged Driving Deaths

The resistance that many people have towards cannabis law reform is fear based. Like a panicky chicken, the prospect of any change at all is met with terror. One of the fears that people have at the thought of cannabis legalisation is that it will lead to carnage on our roads. Like most of the other fears about cannabis law reform, this one is misguided.

As with many of the misgivings that people have about cannabis law reform, the fear of an increase in drugged driving deaths is based on a misconception about how dangerous cannabis is. This is partially based on ignorance, and partially based on the idea that being high on cannabis is like being drunk on alcohol.

The idea seems to be that perfectly otherwise normal people will smoke some cannabis and, because cannabis makes you go crazy, they will get in a car and drive like a crazy person. This perception has been stoked by sensationalist media reporting involving headlines such as "Stoned driver faces jail (1)" when the driver in question had also been smoking methamphetamine.

The idea that cannabis legalisation will lead to more road deaths is not accurate for three major reasons.

The first is that it ignores the substitution effect (for the sake of argument, let's agree here with the lazy assumption that legal cannabis will lead to more use). An individual driving under the influence of cannabis might not be as safe as a sober person. But evidence from elsewhere shows that, if cannabis was legalised, a proportion of incidents of drunk driving will be replaced with incidents of stoned driving, which are safer.

Research has shown that rates of alcohol use fall in places where recreational cannabis is made legal (2). This is because cannabis and alcohol serve as substitutes to a large extent. Because rates of alcohol use fall after cannabis legalisation, rates of drunk driving also fall, and this means that traffic fatalities also fall – significantly.

It's better for a driver to be sober, but if they aren't going to be sober, it's better for them to be stoned than to be drunk. It's a grim calculus, but if legalising cannabis would lead to twenty extra drugged driving deaths at the same time as preventing fifty drunk driving deaths, it would be a worthwhile move.

The second is that the actual science is inconclusive as to whether being stoned impairs driving safety (3). Various studies have provided contradictory results (4). The lazy assumption is that being under the influence of any psychoactive drug, including cannabis, will make a person worse at driving. The reality is that stoned drivers take a variety of measures to reduce their risk of crashing.

Part of the problem is that unregulated cannabis contains a great variety of various cannabinoids, and these cannabinoids can be present at a great variety of frequencies. Studies appear to be clear that high doses of THC impair driver safety (5), which follows logically from the fact that THC is known to have a psychotogenic effect, but there is no such evidence suggesting the same about high doses of CBD.

It also appears to be true that, unlike alcohol, cannabis tolerance has an effect on whether it impairs driving performance (6). For many cannabis users, cannabis is merely a background substance that quietens distracting thoughts. All these reasons mean that, although no responsible person would advocate driving after using cannabis, a person who has just smoked it is not necessarily unsafe to drive.

The third is that it is irrelevant. Like with many arguments against cannabis law reform, focus on the specifics misses the bigger picture.

Not everyone trusts the Government when it says that cannabis is a substance that isn't safe to drive on. As the linked articles above demonstrate, there are indeed instances when a person who has consumed cannabis is not safe to drive. But why would a person trust a Government public safety notice on the subject, when they have previously lied about cannabis full stop?

Over recent decades, governments all over the world have denied that cannabis was medicinal. But because people all over the world knew that it was medicinal, the end result has been decreased trust of governmental pronouncements, particularly when they relate to cannabis. So if a government would give the perfectly reasonable advice to avoid driving within two hours of smoking, it might well be ignored.

If cannabis was legal, and if the Government spoke to the public honestly about it instead of lying, users might trust them when they gave intelligent and prudent advice about smoking cannabis and driving. This would save many more lives in the long run than could possibly be saved by putting cannabis growers and users in prison.

The idea that cannabis legalisation will lead to a spate of fatal traffic accidents is fearmongering. It's the same kind of fearmongering that claimed that legalising homosexuality would lead to everyone dying of AIDS. The experience of overseas territories that have legalised cannabis shows that these fears are little more than hysteria.

# 53

# Reform Doesn't Mean Stoned Workers

One of the most hysterical arguments against cannabis law reform is that it will lead to a spate of workers coming to work stoned. This will be a disaster, we are breathlessly told, because some of these intoxicated workers are responsible for other people's well-being. Such fears are not grounded in reality.

The reasoning seems to be that the nation's workforce cannot handle the temptation of easy access to cannabis, and will inevitably come to start using it all day in the nature of severe drug addicts, such as before work. Images of surgeons giggling maniacally while slicing arteries open are thrown about by pants-pissing old conservatives, who seem to think of cannabis users akin to a horde of zombies.

This argument is false in at least three major ways.

In the first case, people already have access to plenty of legal recreational drugs and choose not to use them. There are a number of industrial jobs that people can't safely do while drunk, and there are a number of customer services roles that can't adequately be performed while stinking of tobacco smoke. In the vast majority of situations, employees in either of these roles don't partake in alcohol or tobacco before work.

If one thinks rationally about the idea, there's no reason to think that legal cannabis would be any different. The case of surgeon is especially ridiculous – surgeon is a professional occupation. The type of person who works in this profession is hardly the sort of person who would experiment with recreational drugs before they go to work anyway.

In the second case, the availability of swab tests that can test for actual cannabis intoxication means that a blanket ban on cannabis is unnecessary. There may have once been a point in such a blanket ban, on account of that there was otherwise no way of telling if a person was dangerously affected by a cannabis high. But accurate swab tests mean that it is no longer necessary to take urine samples (if it ever was).

Most importantly, legal cannabis does not in any sense mean that employers will lose the right to send home workers who are dangerously high. Workers who are intoxicated on any substance, legal or otherwise, are first and foremost a safety risk to other workers and to themselves. So if an employee comes to work stoned, the employer has every right to send them home on the grounds that they are in no state to discharge their duties.

In the third case, the vast majority of cases of cannabis intoxication are immaterial to the job at hand. This is clearly true if one considers that a large number of people who work in roles where attentiveness is paramount are on sedatives, anti-histamines or psychiatric drugs of some kind, and that this is nonetheless acceptable to their employers, who do not drug test them for those substances.

Psychiatric drugs such as Olanzapine have been shown to increase the chance of fatal car accidents (1), and benzodiazepines are even worse. Many people drive while sleepy, and many elderly people are significantly more dangerous behind the wheel than the average driver. If all of these risks come within the bounds of acceptability, then a small amount of cannabis in the system is acceptable as well.

The idea that cannabis law reform would inevitably lead to masses of stoned workers is the kind of overblown hysteria that is typical of cannabis prohibitionists. There are at least three major reasons to think that reform would not impact the safety profile of the workforce. Repealing cannabis prohibition would bring protocol about workplace safety back to sanity and logic.

# 54

# Drugs Are Not Categorically Bad

"Drugs are bad, mmmmmkay?" goes the *South Park* joke. Mr. Garrison's catchphrase satirises the near-total absence of thought that the Establishment has put into their anti-cannabis rhetoric. The idea is that drugs are bad, and cannabis is a drug, therefore cannabis is bad, and therefore cannabis prohibition is justified. As usual, it's not that simple.

The popular conception of what the word "drugs" means is highly variable. Some people consider any foreign substance taken into the body to be drugs. Other people say that anything not prescribed by a doctor is drugs; once it is prescribed it magically becomes medicine. Still others contend that drugs are anything that are bad, and anything not drugs is good.

The kind of person who makes the argument that drugs are categorically bad is usually the sort of person who is obsessed with purity. Inevitably they are a wowser of some kind, and they fit into two categories: the first some kind of physical health freak, the second some kind of religious freak. Their belief is that cannabis disrupts physical and spiritual health, respectively.

The physical truth about many drugs, like most substances that one could put into the body, is that healthy and unhealthy use is a primarily a matter of dosage. The most obvious example is salt, where too much or too little will leave a person in poor health. Some might counter here that a lack of cannabis will not make someone sick, but that's not true in many medicinal cases.

Another example is amphetamines. There are many amphetamines that are basically the same substance as what one finds in ADHD medicines. The major difference is that the crackhead takes it in much, much heavier doses than what a doctor would recommend.

A small amount of cannabis will not hurt a person, unless they are extremely sensitive to smoke or similar. In fact, a small amount might greatly help a person, especially if they suffer from one of the hundreds of different conditions that cannabis is known to treat. By the same token, smoking a hundred joints a day will be bad for you almost without a doubt.

In any case, the fundamental point is that this argument is misdirected. If a particular dose of a particular substance is bad, then don't use it. It's a simple as that!

It's possible that a blanket admonition against drugs along the lines of "drugs are bad" is a good idea if you are a parent speaking to a ten-year old child. Someone without the mental sophistication to make good decisions might need it. But it's no basis for a national law that governs young and old alike.

Adult citizens are not like children, and need to be spoken to honestly. The positive and negative effects of all drugs need to be spoken about honestly, and the citizens need to be informed with reference to reality and science. If this does not happen, then the risk arises that those citizens lose trust in doctors and Government officials, and then movements like the anti-vaxx one start to crop up (1).

Cannabis should not be illegal because "drugs are categorically bad". This is a child's logic, and it should not be informing the national cannabis policy. We need to move on from these simplistic thought patterns, because they do not describe the reality of the situation, and absent that people cannot make correct decisions.

# 55

# Cannabis Does Not Make People Violent

As ridiculous as it may sound to many, the public opinion of cannabis and its effects have been informed by images like the murder scene from *Reefer Madness* (1). In the minds of a large section of the voting-age population, using cannabis leads directly to a desire to murder other people just for the thrill of it, or at least to an meth or alcohol-like aggression. This chapter looks at the truth.

Anyone who has been part of a cannabis-using scene knows that the supposed link between cannabis and violence is bullshit. It's simple enough to just contrast the results of cannabis cafes in Amsterdam, or cannabis festivals, with bars and pubs just about anywhere else. Cannabis, by itself, makes people mellow in the vast majority of cases.

The myth that cannabis makes people violent was proven false as far back as 1977. A review published that year in the *Psychological Bulletin* (2) stated that "The consensus is that marihuana does not precipitate violence in the majority of those using it sporadically or chronically." All of the further research since then backs up this point.

Interestingly, that article cites the importance of set and setting, which is something that any responsible person would emphasise if they wanted to reduce harms (more on this below).

The presence of a scientific consensus that there is no causal link between cannabis use and violence doesn't stop prohibitionists from cherry-picking data and research to create the impression that such a link exists (3). After all, there are correlations between all kinds of things, but (as any honest scientist knows) these correlations are often best explained by underlying third factors.

There is certainly a correlation between violence and cannabis, as there is between violence and everything on the black market. This is inevitable, because anything on the black market is all but guaranteed to be sold by someone who won't go to the Police if they are ripped off, stood over or killed. Cases like the example of Marlborough man Colin Farrell, who was robbed of his cannabis plants in a home invasion (4), only happen because of prohibition.

It's true of everything that if only criminals use it, it will have an association with crime. It's also true that if something is illegal, then only criminals will use it. Therefore, anything that's illegal will have an association with crime. This, by itself, explains most of the link between cannabis and violence.

Another reason why an association exists between cannabis and violence is that some people use cannabis as part of a pattern of polydrug usage during nihilistic benders. There are a lot of meth benders that end up with a person smoking cannabis to try and calm themselves down and get to sleep, only to find it not quite working, at which point something really out of order often happens. The same is true of alcohol benders.

This is why the headlines proclaiming things like "Cannabis Crash Tragedy Kills Five" inevitably lead into an article that describes how the driver was also drunk, and/or on meth and/or on prescription sleeping pills. The mainstream media is happy to play up the cannabis angle to these stories, partly because drink driving fatalities are not news and partly because it pleases the alcohol manufacturers who spend millions advertising in that same media.

Logical thinking tells us that, just because a person smoked cannabis and became violent later doesn't mean that the cannabis caused the violence. This is an example of the informal logical fallacy known as *post hoc ergo propter hoc* (5), or "after this, therefore because of this." This is because people who smoke cannabis and become violent have usually been drinking alcohol or doing methamphetamine at the same time, or haven't slept for days.

Logical thinking would ask: "Where are the cases of murders and violent crimes being committed by people who were only on cannabis and nothing else?"

Of course, there are few or none – even making an Internet search for examples comes up with little. This is because the people who are using cannabis without also using alcohol or methamphetamine are almost always just quietly using it at home, to relax, in a similar manner to how many responsible people drink alcohol daily.

Much like alcohol, the emphasis ought to go on educating people about the real effects of the substance. Absurd lies like the *Reefer Madness* story have to be consigned to history, where they belong alongside witch hunts, virgin sacrifices and the persecution of left-handers as embarrassing examples of human superstition, cowardice and stupidity.

The truth about things like set and setting have to be explained to people, so that they can make intelligent decisions about their cannabis use instead of relying on abstinence-based fearmongering (this is true of alcohol as well as cannabis). Part of this involves only using cannabis in situations where they are safe and where they don't have to be responsible for anything, and preferably around people they like and who won't harass them when they are high.

Any correctly informed person who is concerned about violence would support the legalisation of cannabis, because it would replace known violence-causing drugs (in particular alcohol and methamphetamine) with something that causes less violence. In reality, the connection between cannabis and violence is so weak that, far from being an argument for its prohibition, it's an argument to legalise it.

# 56

# There Is No Moral Argument Against Cannabis

Some cannabis prohibitionists contend that cannabis should remain illegal because its use is immoral. This immorality is such that it's fair to use the criminal justice system to prevent it from happening. As this chapter will examine, not only is there no moral argument against cannabis, but the moral equation suggests that it should be legal.

The sort of person making this argument is usually some kind of wowser. This is the reason why this argument is becoming less common – proponents of it are dying off.

Usually, the argument takes some form of slippery slope argument. The typical form is that smoking cannabis is claimed to lead, by stepwise degeneracy, into the total abandonment of all healthy human values, until the user deteriorates into a wretched shell of the person they once were. Here the spectre of *Reefer Madness* can be seen once again.

The idea that cannabis use is inherently immoral harkens back to the religious fundamentalist idea that all pleasure is inherently sinful, on account of that it induces a person to worship the material world instead of God. It's essentially a religious idea, and fundamentalist in the sense that the suffering caused by this admonition is ignored.

In reality, human beings have a need for recreational activity or they will become mentally ill. This is apparent from observing anywhere in history where those activities have been restricted. Pleasure is not inherently immoral, and it's not immoral to enjoy one's life, provided that one's duties are still met and one's responsibilities still discharged.

To the contrary – there is a moral imperative to enjoy one's life, for if one does not do so, then bitterness, anger, frustration and depression are the consequences. These emotions invariably take themselves out on other people. Therefore, a person has a moral imperative to keep themselves happy enough that they can have a positive effect on other people. If using cannabis helps achieve this, so be it.

Morally speaking, the correct course of action to take at any given time is the one that minimises the suffering of conscious beings. It isn't to blindly follow the law, and neither is it to blindly follow some crude ascetic concept of religious purity by banning and avoiding all recreational substances. If such a thing could be summarised, we might say that it's closer to taking the correct decision in every situation, despite the pressures and temptations to take the wrong one.

Some might argue that people have more important things to do than to use cannabis. That's all well and good, but it isn't a sufficient argument to make cannabis illegal. It's entirely possible that some people use cannabis when they could have been doing something more edifying or productive. This would still not constitute a moral demand to attack these people through the criminal justice system.

Others might argue that the moral imperative lies not with the prospective cannabis user, but with society, who ought to act to make cannabis less widely available. But this, too, is an example of putting abstract rules ahead of a sober calculation of which legal arrangement leads to the least suffering. Punishing cannabis suppliers and users cannot be the way forward.

It can hardly be argued that setting the Police and the criminal justice system onto someone for growing or using cannabis is the morally correct thing to do. The effect of being arrested and potentially dragged through court is more suffering than could ever possibly be prevented by breaking a cannabis habit. If moral considerations are important, then we need to look for a less brutal solution.

The most morally sophisticated way of dealing with cannabis is to make it legal, and to use some of the money freed up by this to fix any problem that might arise. It is estimated that legalising cannabis could save even a small country like New Zealand up to $500 million per year (1). This would provide ample funding to every drug counselling service in the whole country.

If this was coupled with a cultural change that saw cannabis dependency treated like dependency for legal drugs, instead of a moral failure for which one must be punished, it might be possible to encourage people who were dependent to get help instead of intending to force them away from cannabis by using the Police and prisons. If there is a moral argument around cannabis, that is surely the solution.

# 57

# Cannabis Is An Exit Drug

Many people erroneously believe that cannabis is a "gateway drug" that leads to users moving on to harder and harder drugs. The reality, like many myths relating to cannabis, is closer to the opposite of this. Cannabis can actually serve as an 'exit drug' to help people overcome addictions to actually harmful substances, in particular alcohol, synthetics and opioids.

In New Zealand, there is a "synthetic cannabis" epidemic underway. A couple of recent deaths in Christchurch were believed to have been caused by the substances (1), and the total number of deaths in New Zealand this year attributed to them is approaching 50 (2). This is rightly a public health crisis, and is increasingly being understood as such.

The substances being sold as synthetic cannabis generally have nothing to do with cannabis (3) – they are mostly unknown psychoactives that generate some kind of buzz when smoked. No-one's really sure where they come from or what's in them, they're just sold through shady contacts – often at tinny houses when someone was looking for natural cannabis – and end up killing people in the streets.

It doesn't matter that these substances aren't really much like cannabis, because they fill a market niche that would otherwise be filled by cannabis. If a person doesn't like to drink alcohol, for whatever reason, the major alternative is some form of cannabis. If cannabis is not available, because prohibition has made it impossible to supply it, then "synthetic cannabis" might have to do, because it will frequently be available through the same channels that a person would try to access natural cannabis.

For the many thousands of Kiwis believed to be addicted to synthetic cannabis, and for the hundreds of thousands who are at risk of encountering some synnies from one of the infamous "bad batches" that kill people from time to time, legal cannabis could serve as an exit drug (4). With legal cannabis in place, even if only at the medicinal level, a synthetic cannabis addict could be weaned off the synnies with a replacement medicinal cannabis regimen.

In America, there is an opioid epidemic underway (5). Opioid overdoses were believed to comprise 49,000 of the 72,000 drug overdose deaths in America in 2017. This contrasts with about 10,000 such deaths at the turn of the century. This represents several times more deaths than even the infamous American homicide rate – clearly a crisis of such proportions that extraordinary actions must now be considered.

Cannabis has shown immense promise as an exit drug from opioid addiction. *Science Daily* links a report from the University of British Colombia (6) that found significant evidence to suggest that cannabis can help in the case of alcoholism and opiate addiction. There are already clinics in operation in Los Angeles where cannabis is part of a program of rehabilitation from heroin and alcohol misuse (7).

A study in the *Journal of the American Medical Association* (8) found that rates of opioid use are lower in American states that have legalised medicinal cannabis (9), which suggests that individuals who use opiates are happy to wean themselves off them by using cannabis, if only they are given the opportunity. The *JAMA* study found that "States with medical cannabis laws had a 24.8% lower mean annual opioid overdose mortality rate compared with states without medical cannabis laws."

A report by *Time* magazine found that rates of death by opioid overdose had quadrupled from the turn of the century (10), and that states which had legalised medicinal cannabis had saved hundreds of millions of dollars from alleviating some amount of opioid abuse. Even if a patient does not stop taking opiates completely, it is possible that a synergistic effect from the cannabis can potentiate the opiates they do take, meaning that they can take less for the same painkiller effect.

All this means that cannabis prohibition is effectively killing people, by preventing those addicted to alcohol and opiates from accessing a potential exit drug, and thereby forcing them to remain addicted to the substance.

Despite the apparent moralistic intent behind cannabis prohibition, we can safely suggest that the spirit of the law was not that it should kill alcoholics and opioid addicts.

Cannabis law reform is necessary so that medicinal cannabis can be applied as an exit drug to people who are addicted to, or dependent on, more harmful substances. This will have the effect of substituting a substance that heals for substances that harm, and thereby preventing suffering.

# 58

# Prohibition Does Not Serve The Good Of Society

Cannabis prohibitionists have a fallback position when none of the usual rhetoric succeeds. It's a vague appeal to some kind of "good of society". This argument encompasses a variety of different sentiments, most of them fear-based. As this chapter will examine, this argument is no more true than any of the others.

At the time this chapter was being composed, it was in the news that a Dunedin man named Harley Brown had just been sentenced to two years and three months in prison for growing over a hundred cannabis plants (1). Meanwhile, another man named John-Boy Rakete had been sentenced, two weeks previously, to two years and two months in prison for bashing a man into a coma from which he is expected to never recover (2).

Imagine going to prison for growing a medicinal flower at the same time as a gang member who beat someone into a vegetable state, and seeing that gang member get out of prison before you. It sounds like something out of a Kafka novel, but it's the reality of our current legal approach to cannabis. Can it fairly be argued that this arrangement serves the good of society?

It's hard to see where the benefit to society is in this arrangement. Brown will be incarcerated at the cost of $100,000 per year, which is greater than the total value of the cannabis plants he had, even if this value is calculated using Police maths. As a result of his incarceration, a number of people will be made to suffer without the medicine they would otherwise have had.

How does this serve the good of society?

Rather than serving the good of society, prohibition puts us at each other's throats. The friends and family of Harley Brown will probably have contempt for the system for the rest of their lives. Most people who compare the two cases above and their respective sentences will conclude that something is fundamentally rotten with our justice system, which appears to dish out punishments with no consideration given to how much suffering the perpetrator may have caused.

The good of society is served by alleviating the suffering of the people in that society. Education is a public good because ignorance causes suffering. Healthcare is a public good because disease causes suffering. Infrastructure is a public good because mobility restrictions cause suffering. Anything that is genuinely a public good alleviates suffering somewhere.

Prohibition serves no such good. As has been demonstrated in the previous chapters of this book, it doesn't prevent suffering, but, to the contrary, it causes suffering. There is no social good served by arresting people who aren't harming any one. Neither is any good served by imprisoning these people. Least of all is any good served by lying about how cannabis causes harm to the community when it's really a medicine.

The ultimate reason why cannabis prohibition does not serve the good of society is that the people will never accept not being allowed to use cannabis. The people will always intuitively feel that they have the right to use cannabis, because it alleviates suffering, because it's a social tonic and because it can connect people to God. Because of this, prohibition can only ever cause conflict between the people and those tasked with enforcing it.

The idea that people will eventually "come to their senses", realise that cannabis is a dangerous drug, and stop using it, is nonsense. Cannabis prohibitionists have gone all-in on this puritanical delusion, and they have lost. It's time to admit that reality does not reflect the idea that cannabis is dangerous, or that the harms of cannabis are in any way ameliorated by making it illegal.

The good of society is best served by honesty. Honesty is one of the most fundamental virtues, because it's only through honest discussion that we can come to see the world accurately. Without being able to see the world accurately, we will make mistakes that lead to conflict.

This honesty would cause us to have a look at Colorado, where they legalised cannabis in 2014. In Colorado, none of the terrible things that the prohibitionists predicted came to pass. There wasn't an outbreak of violence or other crimes, there wasn't an epidemic of cannabis addiction and it didn't become easier for young people to get. Everything continued the same as normal, only there was much more money on account of it no longer being wasted on enforcing prohibition.

Legalisation would serve the good of society much better than prohibition. A system of legal cannabis would not only increase social cohesion by removing one of the major wedges that drives us apart, but it would also increase the respect that the average person has for the Police, the Justice System and the Government. Not least of all, it would save us a ton of money.

# 59

# References

**1    Prohibition Doesn't Work**

1    https://en.wikipedia.org/wiki/Annual_cannabis_use_by_country

2    http://vjmpublishing.nz/?p=10600

3    https://en.wikipedia.org/wiki/Harry_J._Anslinger

4    https://en.wikipedia.org/wiki/Timeline_of_cannabis_law


**2    The Market Needs To Be Regulated**

1    http://vjmpublishing.nz/?p=10477


**5    Cannabis Is A Medicine**

1    https://www.bmj.com/content/365/bmj.l1903

2    https://www.onlinepot.org/medical/Dr_Tods_PDFs/s3_3.pdf

3    https://www.sciencedirect.com/science/article/pii/S0378874118316611

4    https://www.cambridge.org/core/journals/the-british-journal-of-psychiatry/article/therapeutic-aspects-of-cannabis-and-cannabinoids/A6F35FDD2868806FD91F0F215B24736C

5    https://www.sciencedirect.com/science/article/pii/S1542356513006046

6    https://www.pharmaceutical-journal.com/opinion/insight/medical-cannabis-evidence-challenges-and-barriers-to-progress/20205376.article

7    https://www.fasebj.org/doi/abs/10.1096/fj.00-0399fje

8    https://www.liebertpub.com/doi/full/10.1089/can.2017.0059

9    https://www.liebertpub.com/doi/abs/10.1089/jpm.2018.0529

10    https://www.ncbi.nlm.nih.gov/pmc/articles/PMC6326553/

11    https://www.bmj.com/content/365/bmj.l1141.full

12  https://open-access.imh.com.sg/bitstream/123456789/5182/1/9%20Cannabis%20in%20the%20Treatment%20of%20Mental%20Health.pdf

13  https://www.ncbi.nlm.nih.gov/pmc/articles/PMC3763649/

14  https://www.ncbi.nlm.nih.gov/pmc/articles/PMC5312634/

15  https://www.ingentaconnect.com/content/wk/cjpn/2016/00000032/00000012/art00003

16  https://scholarworks.waldenu.edu/dissertations/6804/

17  http://vjmpublishing.nz/?p=7804

18  https://allafrica.com/stories/201904100840.html

## 6  Cannabis Is An Established Crop

1  https://www.denverpost.com/2018/02/10/colorado-pot-sales-2017-border-towns/

## 7  Effectiveness Of The Police

1  https://www.independent.co.uk/news/uk/politics/legalise-cannabis-lib-dems-million-police-hours-wasted-general-election-2017-latest-a7733191.html

## 8  Prohibition Is A Waste Of Money

1  https://assets.documentcloud.org/documents/2995244/Bill-English-Cannabis-OIA.pdf

2  https://www.cato.org/publications/white-paper/budgetary-impact-ending-drug-prohibition

3  https://www.radionz.co.nz/news/political/375375/regulating-cannabis-could-generate-240m-in-tax-report

4  https://www.colorado.gov/pacific/revenue/colorado-marijuana-sales-reports

## 9  Prohibition Harms Respect For The Law And For The Police

1  http://vjmpublishing.nz/?p=1372

2  http://vjmpublishing.nz/?p=5374

## 10  The Punishment Does Not Fit The Crime

1:  http://www.legislation.govt.nz/act/public/1975/0116/82.0/DLM436239.html

2:  https://www.stuff.co.nz/auckland/local-news/northland/98764492/jail-for-daktory-cannabis-founder

3:  https://www.stuff.co.nz/national/crime/108861942/auckland-youth-worker-who-groomed-12yearold-girl-sentenced-to-home-detention

4:   https://www.stuff.co.nz/nelson-mail/news/107897285/takaka-mother-sent-to-prison-for-causing-fatal-new-years-eve-crash-while-on-meth

5:   http://www.legislation.govt.nz/act/public/1975/0116/82.0/DLM436264.html

## 12  Cannabis Is An Alternative To Booze

1   https://www.pmgt.org.nz/alcohol/

2   https://www.hpa.org.nz/sites/default/files/imported/field_research_publication_file/BurdenFull.pdf

3   http://rogersandmoss.com/blog/14-criminal-law-articles/56-two-years-later-has-the-legalization-of-marijuana-affected-crime-in-colorado

4   http://vjmpublishing.nz/?p=7804

## 13  Other Acceptable Drugs Are More Harmful

1   https://www.alcohol.org.nz/resources-research/facts-and-statistics/nz-statistics/health-injury

2   https://www.health.govt.nz/your-health/healthy-living/addictions/smoking/health-effects-smoking

## 14  Prohibition Harms Minorities

1   https://collections.concourt.org.za/bitstream/handle/20.500.12144/34547/Full%20judgment%20Official%20version%2018%20September%202018.pdf

## 15  It's Easier To Stop Using Cannabis If It's Legal

1   http://vjmpublishing.nz/?p=12374

2   https://www.verywellmind.com/variable-interval-schedule-2796011

3   https://www.verywellmind.com/what-is-a-fixed-interval-schedule-2795189

## 16  Prohibition Harms The Youth

1   https://dataunodc.un.org/drugs/prevalence_youth

2   https://www.scientificamerican.com/article/colorado-s-teen-marijuana-usage-dips-after-legalization/

3   https://www.denverpost.com/2016/06/20/marijuana-use-colorado-teens-marijuana-no-increase/

## 17  An Elderly Perspective

1   http://vjmpublishing.nz/?p=2823

2   https://www.sciencedirect.com/science/article/pii/S0953620518300190

3   https://journals.lww.com/clinicalneuropharm/Abstract/2017/11000/Medical_
Cannabis_in_Parkinson_Disease___Real_Life.8.aspx

4   https://journals.sagepub.com/doi/abs/10.1177/0269881117699616

5   https://www.cfp.ca/content/61/8/e372.short

6   https://europepmc.org/articles/pmc6326663

7   https://patents.google.com/patent/US20180104213A1/en

8   https://www.sciencedirect.com/science/article/abs/pii/S0378512218306868

9   https://www.ncbi.nlm.nih.gov/pmc/articles/PMC6024284/

**19 Prohibition Funds Crime**

1   https://www.health.govt.nz/publication/research-report-new-zealand-drug-harm-
index-2016

**20 It Doesn't Matter That Awful People Support Cannabis Law Reform**

1   http://vjmpublishing.nz/?p=3346

2   http://vjmpublishing.nz/?p=11562

3   https://yourlogicalfallacyis.com/ad-hominem

**21 Law Reform Is Not A 'Slippery Slope'**

1   https://yourlogicalfallacyis.com/slippery-slope

**22 Cannabis Is A Religious And Spiritual Sacrament**

1   https://en.wikipedia.org/wiki/Cannabis_in_India

2   https://www.cannabis.info/en/blog/sadhus-indian-holy-men-unique-link

3   https://en.wikipedia.org/wiki/Maha_Shivaratri

4   https://en.wikipedia.org/wiki/Entheogenic_use_of_cannabis

5   http://herbmuseum.ca/content/scythians-cannabis

6   https://culturemagazine.com/vikings-and-cannabis/

7   https://tokinwoman.blogspot.com/2016/10/viking-volvas-and-cannabis-seeds.html

**24 Quality Control**

1   https://livingcheapinnorway.com/2018/12/15/staying-in-norway-on-a-budget-
alcohol/

2   https://www.ncbi.nlm.nih.gov/pmc/articles/PMC6143823/

## 26  Prohibition Harms Social Cohesion

1    http://vjmpublishing.nz/?p=3346

## 27  Governments Shouldn't Conduct Wars Against Their Own People

1    https://en.wikipedia.org/wiki/United_States_incarceration_rate

2    https://www.nap.edu/read/18613/chapter/3

3    https://harpers.org/archive/2016/04/legalize-it-all/

## 28  Prohibition Corrupts The Youth

1    http://vjmpublishing.nz/?p=5090

## 30  Cannabis Is Not A Gateway Drug

1    http://vjmpublishing.nz/?p=9919

## 31  Legalisation Would Not Increase Rates Of Cannabis Use

1    http://vjmpublishing.nz/?p=11161

2    http://vjmpublishing.nz/?p=12120

3    https://en.wikipedia.org/wiki/Annual_cannabis_use_by_country

4    https://www.scientificamerican.com/article/colorado-s-teen-marijuana-usage-dips-after-legalization/

5    https://www.washingtonpost.com/news/wonk/wp/2017/12/11/following-marijuana-legalization-teen-drug-use-is-down-in-colorado/

## 33  Prohibition Raises Prices But Also Raises Incentive To Supply

1    https://en.wikipedia.org/wiki/Risk_premium

2    https://marijuanarates.com/blog/colorado-marijuana-prices

3    http://www.priceofweed.com/prices/United-States/Washington.html

4    https://www.businessinsider.com.au/washington-state-survey-shows-marijuana-legalization-didnt-affect-teen-use-rates-2017-3

5    https://www.independent.co.uk/life-style/health-and-families/health-news/the-7-charts-that-show-the-countries-with-the-highest-number-of-teenage-cannabis-smokers-a6932261.html

## 35  Legalisation Will Not Lead To A Black Market

1    https://en.wikipedia.org/wiki/Risk_premium

2    https://www.theguardian.com/world/2013/oct/22/uruguay-legal-cannabis-1-dollar-gram

3    https://www.stuff.co.nz/the-press/84577938/tobacco-black-market-grows-as-tax-increases-hit-home

## 36  Cannabis Is Not Harmful

1    http://www.police.govt.nz/advice/drugs-and-alcohol/illicit-drugs-offences-and-penalties

2    https://www.cambridge.org/core/journals/psychological-medicine/article/psychotic-patients-who-used-cannabis-frequently-before-illness-onset-have-higher-genetic-predisposition-to-schizophrenia-than-those-who-did-not/4-6CC7A5C04C0AC761B144A613B4254C8#

## 39  Cannabis Is Not Addictive

1    https://link.springer.com/article/10.1007/s11481-018-9782-9

2    https://www.tandfonline.com/doi/full/10.1080/08897077.2015.1023484

3    https://link.springer.com/chapter/10.1007/978-3-319-90365-1_11

4    https://www.psychologytoday.com/us/blog/reading-between-the-headlines/201205/is-marijuana-addictive

5    https://www.recoveryranch.com/articles/mortality-rates-alcohol-withdrawal/

6    https://en.wikipedia.org/wiki/Rat_Park#Rat_Park_experiments

## 40  Cannabis Does Not Cause Schizophrenia

1    http://vjmpublishing.nz/?p=4855

2    https://academic.oup.com/schizophreniabulletin/article-abstract/44/1/18/4804576

3    https://www.sciencedirect.com/science/article/pii/B978012804791000001X

4    https://academic.oup.com/schizophreniabulletin/article/44/suppl_1/S27/4957129

5    https://www.liebertpub.com/doi/abs/10.1089/can.2016.0036

6    https://ajp.psychiatryonline.org/doi/abs/10.1176/appi.ajp.2017.17030325

7    https://www.cambridge.org/core/journals/psychological-medicine/article/assessing-causality-in-associations-between-cannabis-use-and-schizophrenia-risk-a-twosample-mendelian-randomization-study/122D651C3670683DAEDDA33997417105

8    https://www.biorxiv.org/content/early/2018/01/08/234294

9    http://stm.sciencemag.org/content/10/460/eaav0342

10   https://www.sciencedirect.com/science/article/pii/S0376871616309292

11   http://vjmpublishing.nz/?p=10288

## 42  Cannabis Does Not Make People Impotent

1   https://link.springer.com/chapter/10.1007/3-7643-7358-X_1

2   http://www.scielo.br/scielo.php?pid=S1516-44462006000200015&script=sci_arttext&tlng=pt

3   http://vjmpublishing.nz/?p=480


## 43  Amotivational Syndrome Is Not Reason To Prohibit Cannabis

1   https://www.tandfonline.com/doi/abs/10.1080/02791072.1983.10471963

2   https://nyaspubs.onlinelibrary.wiley.com/doi/pdf/10.1111/j.1749-6632.1976.tb49881.x

3   http://vjmpublishing.nz/?p=3347


## 44  Cannabis Does Not Lead To Crime

1   https://www.nzherald.co.nz/nz/news/article.cfm?c_id=1&objectid=12140895

2   https://www.forbes.com/sites/janetwburns/2018/01/16/violent-crime-has-fallen-in-border-states-with-legal-cannabis-study/#11da244d59eb


## 45  It Doesn't Matter That High-THC Strains Now Exist

1   https://www.bbc.com/news/health-43196566

2   https://www.ncbi.nlm.nih.gov/pubmed/22716160


## 46  It Doesn't Matter That People Have To Pay For Cannabis Users' Healthcare

1   https://www.alcohol.org.nz/sites/default/files/documents/Alcohol%20Quickfact%20Facts_0.pdf

2   https://www.health.govt.nz/system/files/documents/publications/nz-drug-harm-index-2016-2nd-ed-jul16.pdf

3   https://www.nzherald.co.nz/nz/news/article.cfm?c_id=1&objectid=10517995

4   http://theconversation.com/new-zealands-health-service-performs-well-but-inequities-remain-high-82648

5   https://www.health.govt.nz/nz-health-statistics/health-statistics-and-data-sets/older-peoples-health-data-and-stats/dhb-spending-services-older-people


## 47  Legalisation Is Better For The Environment

1   http://www.lifeworth.com/deepadaptation.pdf

2   https://www.theguardian.com/us-news/2016/feb/27/marijuana-industry-huge-energy-footprint

## 48  A Majority Now Want Reform

1  https://news.gallup.com/poll/1657/illegal-drugs.aspx

2  https://en.wikipedia.org/wiki/1996_California_Proposition_215

3  https://www.independent.co.uk/news/uk/home-news/cannabis-legalisation-uk-public-support-yougov-survey-marijuana-rob-wilson-a9004101.html

4  https://en.wikipedia.org/wiki/New_Zealand_cannabis_referendum

5  https://www.drugfoundation.org.nz/news-media-and-events/new-survey-results-show-legal-cannabis-a-real-possibility/

6  http://vjmpublishing.nz/?p=3346

## 49  One Person Who Smoked Cannabis And Went Crazy Is Not A Pattern

1  https://www.health.govt.nz/publication/cannabis-use-2012-13-new-zealand-health-survey

## 50  Fears of A 'Big Cannabis' Lobby Are Overblown

1  https://news.gallup.com/poll/7270/most-smokers-wish-they-could-quit.aspx

## 52  Legalisation Would Not Increase Drugged Driving Deaths

1  https://www.stuff.co.nz/taranaki-daily-news/news/68171779

2  https://www.journals.uchicago.edu/doi/10.1086/668812

3  https://www.tandfonline.com/doi/abs/10.1080/10550490902786934

4  https://www.theverge.com/2019/2/5/18210827/marijuana-traffic-fatality-deaths-transportation-public-health

5  https://onlinelibrary.wiley.com/doi/abs/10.1111/fcp.12382

6  http://clinchem.aaccjnls.org/content/early/2019/03/05/clinchem.2018.299727.abstract

## 53  Reform Doesn't Mean Stoned Workers

1  https://bottomlineinc.com/health/medications/drugs-that-increase-the-risk-for-car-crashes

## 54  Drugs Are Not Categorically Bad

1  http://vjmpublishing.nz/?p=2862

## 55  Cannabis Does Not Make People Violent

1  https://www.youtube.com/watch?v=vtngFEE5t1E

2  https://psycnet.apa.org/record/1977-27069-001

3   https://www.stuff.co.nz/national/health/112765917/alison-mau-family-first-is-trying-to-scare-you--dont-fall-for-it

4   https://www.stuff.co.nz/national/crime/98856368/pair-jailed-for-attack-on-dying-man-blame-german-muscle-for-violence

5   https://en.wikipedia.org/wiki/Post_hoc_ergo_propter_hoc

## 56  There Is No Moral Argument Against Cannabis

1   https://www.stuff.co.nz/business/industries/109443403/cannabis-legalisation-in-new-zealand-could-bring-in-up-to-240m-in-tax-revenue-economist-says

## 57  Cannabis Is An Exit Drug

1   https://www.stuff.co.nz/the-press/news/107560205/Health-minister-wants-synthetic-cannabis-reclassified-after-Christchurch-death

2   https://www.theguardian.com/world/2018/jul/27/synthetic-cannabis-deaths-new-zealand-legalisation-debate

3   https://www.drugs.com/illicit/synthetic-marijuana.html

4   http://blog.eternalvigilance.me/2014/03/the-exit-drug-cannabis/

5   https://en.wikipedia.org/wiki/Opioid_epidemic

6   https://www.sciencedaily.com/releases/2016/11/161116102847.htm

7   https://cannabismd.com/health/addiction/la-rehab-center-cannabis-exit-drug/

8   https://jamanetwork.com/journals/jamainternalmedicine/fullarticle/1898878

9   https://www.adn.com/opinions/2018/06/03/cannabis-is-the-exit-drug/

10  http://time.com/4419003/can-medical-marijuana-help-end-the-opioid-epidemic/

## 58  Prohibition Does Not Serve The Good of Society

1   https://www.odt.co.nz/news/dunedin/cannabis-grower-driven-profit

2   https://www.nzherald.co.nz/nz/news/article.cfm?c_id=1&objectid=12245065

# Also by VJM Publishing:

*Best of VJMP 2018* is a collection of the greatest hits from the VJM Publishing company page during 2018. These essays and articles are the most powerful hits of pure truth you can buy in today's information marketplace.

*Best of VJMP 2017* is a compilation of the most excellent, ballsy and triggering essays published on the VJM Publishing home page during the year of 2017. They cover all kinds of subjects, both mystical and profane, from a Kiwi alt-centrist perspective.

Vince McLeod's *The Verity Key* is a New Zealand cyberpunk novel about a young virtual reality fighting champion who finds himself drawn into the saga of a device that can control the thoughts of other people by satellite.

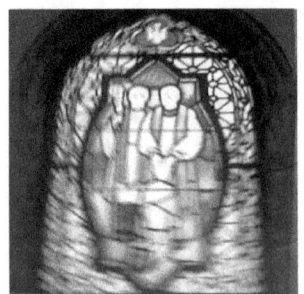

Colin Craic's *The Book of Faith* is a satirical book about honest ways to accrue faith in the modern religious marketplace, and how many things generally considered bad are really good once the power of faith transforms your perspective.

Dan McGlashan's *Understanding New Zealand* is the complete statistical guide to the voting patterns and demographics of the New Zealand people.

Simon P. Murphy's *His Master's Wretched Organ* is a collection of New Zealand short stories that probe themes of disconnection, self-inquiry, spiritual ascendancy, awe and horror.

*Learn Spanish Vocabulary With Mnemonics* uses mnemonics to teach Spanish vocabulary as quickly and efficiently as possible. Some of the mnemonics are weird, some sexy, some cheerfully obscene, but all are memorable.

Anna Nilsen's *Writing with the I Ching* is about using the 64 Hexagrams of the ancient Chinese divination system to inspire your creative writing. Book 4 in the *Writing With Psychology* series.

**For more see www.vjmpublishing.nz**